The Secret Life of
LEINSTER HOUSE

Gavan Reilly is political correspondent for Virgin Media News, and a co-host of its popular podcast, *The Group Chat*. He is one of Ireland's most recognisable broadcasters, and a regular contributor to television and radio programmes across the island. He is also a regular presenter of *The Tonight Show* and has hosted marquee programmes on Newstalk and Today FM. From Meath, he lives in Dublin with his wife Ciara and their two daughters, Doireann and Bláthnaid.

The Secret Life of

LEINSTER HOUSE

GAVAN REILLY

What you *really* need
to know about how
the country is run

Gill Books

Gill Books
Hume Avenue
Park West
Dublin 12
www.gillbooks.ie

Gill Books is an imprint of M.H. Gill and Co.

9781804583265
Designed by Padraig McCormack
Edited by Esther Ní Dhonnacha
Proofread by Liza Costello
Printed and bound in Great Britain by Clays Ltd, Elcograf S.p.A.
This book is typeset in 12pt on 16pt, Adobe Garamond Pro

*The paper used in this book comes from the
wood pulp of sustainably managed forests.*

*To the best of our knowledge, this book complies in full with the requirements
of the General Product Safety Regulation (GPSR). For further information
and help with any safety queries, please contact us at productsafety@gill.ie.*

A CIP catalogue record for this book is available from the British Library.

5 4 3 2 1

To Ciara, Doireann and Bláthnaid,
my three favourite people.

1

PUSH AND PULL

Much about Leinster House is accidental. Even its use as the primary venue of Irish politics was an accident. When Ireland won independence in 1921, the country had no ready-made venue for its new parliament to sit; the building was rented from the Royal Dublin Society simply so that the octagonal lecture theatre could be repurposed as a seated chamber for Dáil Éireann. Even more accidentally, the building was literally the home of one Irish politician in the past: Leinster House (and Kildare Street) are named after the Fitzgerald family, the Earls of Kildare and later the Dukes of Leinster. While the Fitzgeralds were mostly based in Carton House outside Maynooth, Leinster House was the urban residence they used when the Irish parliament was in session at nearby College Green, in what is now a Bank of Ireland. Its illustrious owners were not convinced about its ability to fire the synapses. 'Leinster House,' Lord Edward Fitzgerald once wrote, 'does not inspire the brightest ideas.' (The US President John F. Kennedy recited this line, apparently jokingly, when he addressed a joint sitting of the Dáil and Seanad in 1963. The remark having caused some inadvertent upset to his hosts, either Kennedy or his Irish counterpart Eamon de Valera had the sentence clipped from the official videotape of the speech.)

Depending on who you ask, Edward Fitzgerald was either not cut out for politics, or a soothsayer who realised very early that the mansion on Merrion Square was perhaps not the workplace most conducive to the conception of big ideas. For better or worse, however, it is where those ideas are supposed to find their genesis.

'The first time you get into the Dáil chamber,' one TD recalls, 'you're struck by the shape of it. The ceiling is much taller than you think, but the floor is much flatter, and the furniture is all wooden. The acoustics are woeful: if there's any kind of murmuring, or heckling, it can actually be really hard to hear someone on the other side of the chamber.

'Which, in fairness, does make you wonder if we're really working in the best possible place.'

ʒ

Those who enter politics are either pulled, or pushed, into it. While almost all are in the game in pursuit of what they see as the betterment of Ireland, everyone's path is different. Some feel compelled into the public realm by a sincerely held cause, becoming figureheads for that cause and sent to Leinster House as the ambassador of their movement. Others are motivated by a personal grievance and, in engaging with the system as citizens, find themselves stimulated by learning the structures of systems and where to push for change. Some work for years knocking on doors, running in every available election, ultimately hoping to break the dam and win a seat. Others are approached with an invitation to run.

The paths into politics are many, and merely being of civic mind does not always guarantee getting there. Wanting to enter politics, and actually choosing to pursue a political career, are two very different things.

What makes them do it? The pay might be good, but the job security is woeful, and the working conditions are often punitive. Many are constantly looking over their shoulders wondering when the next election will be, or fretting about the need to fundraise so that there is adequate cash in the bank for the fight whenever it comes. Many with ministries are wondering if they can hang on; many without are wondering if a promotion might ever come their way.

Sometimes, as the author was surprised to learn in the course of interviews for this book, even ministers themselves are yearning for a way out, drained by the job yet terrified of admitting – after climbing so high up the ladder – that they no longer want to be there.

Even some TDs from political families never intended to be there at all. Marc MacSharry of Sligo is the youngest of the six children of Ray MacSharry, who spent a quarter of a century in public life as a TD, minister, tánaiste, MEP and European Commissioner. But if any of the six were to follow their father into political life, it seemed more likely it would be the eldest, Heather Ann, who went into business and became a distinguished figure on several major corporate and financial boards. Marc served on Fianna Fáil's national youth committee during his college years but never considered it as a full-time profession, in part because Fianna Fáil already held a relatively 'safe' seat in Sligo town.

After going into business as a meat exporter, he was eventually pulled into politics when he was approached by Chambers Ireland, the nationwide umbrella group of chambers of commerce. The 2002 Seanad elections were approaching, and the group was entitled to nominate a candidate. MacSharry was chief executive of the chamber of commerce in Sligo town and was asked if he'd consider putting his name forward. Within weeks he'd been elected to the Seanad and went on to spend over two decades in Leinster House as a senator and then TD.

'Sometimes it pisses you off,' he says, 'when you're listening to this nepotism bullshit that people talk about in politics – nobody hands anybody any seat, ever. And being somebody's son or nephew can be a liability, believe it or not. So, you know, maybe at a very early age I was saying, "God, I wouldn't mind doing what my dad is doing," or whatever, but that's not the way the career went. So it happened sort of organically, and almost by accident.'

Not everyone would share MacSharry's view that a family history in politics is a liability. Name recognition for politicians is an enormous asset; most are of the belief that simply having the reputation of being 'a long-standing public rep in this area' is an inherent boost when the next election comes around. If someone has been a TD for ages, their supposition goes, a passive voter must conclude that they have been continually doing a good enough job. Having a family link to a previous office-holder, by extension, allows a new candidate to campaign with the aura of carrying the torch and the presumption that they have learned the trade at their older relative's knee.

MacSharry's own approach to politics may have been coloured by having seen the pressures placed on his own father. The highest offices had little lustre when Marc had grown up behind the scenes. Politics and politicians were so scarcely resourced at the time that TDs simply didn't have a budget to open separate constituency offices and did almost all the work from home. 'I remember clinics on a Saturday: all day Saturday, you'd have two or three hundred people queuing to see the auld fella with whatever issues that there may have been. One of my older siblings would be getting twenty pence to sit inside the front door of the house reading a book, so that they could open the door every time it rang and show people in – making people sit into one room where he was seeing people in the other.'

Nor is he convinced that, despite what many people say, politics today is any more inhospitable than in his father's day. 'This is a tough business, as is the retail business, as is the hospitality business, where hostility and abuse flow. Now, death threats and all of those things? Of course, we should be condemning them.

But I do feel the difficulty of political business at the moment' – threats to politicians' personal safety, or the intensity of criticism that can be directed at them – 'is overstated.'

The reward, in MacSharry's eyes, is simply being able to improve things: to secure better infrastructure, to bring more visitors, to pursue big ideas to fruition.

ȣ

Others are born nowhere near such dynastic backgrounds. Fine Gael's Noel Rock was raised in a troubled part of Finglas with plenty of social difficulty and was attracted to participative politics by realising that only national action could make meaningful inroads into urban disadvantage in areas like the one where he grew up. 'For all its flaws – and there are many – it's still the most practical way to make a real difference to your community and the only way to make a real difference to legislation,' he says. 'Having seen it from many perspectives, while there are better-paid ways to work on policy outside of politics, you will always ultimately have to engage with the political system and the systems of governance. Representative politics is where you have to be if your goal is to bring about positive change.' This meant getting involved in Young Fine Gael during his time studying in DCU, running for Dublin City Council for the first time aged 21, and working diligently to build up the party's presence in working-class areas that had not traditionally supported a mercantile, pro-enterprise party like Fine Gael. Eventually he secured a council seat in 2014, and a Dáil seat in 2016 – the first time in 20 years that Fine Gael took a seat in Dublin North-West. Politics for him was not an accidental pursuit: nobody came knocking on his door inviting him to take a seat. Winning over enough voters to get elected was the work of almost a decade.

His party colleague Brendan Griffin grew up in a household that had a keen interest in public affairs, but no major political loyalty. 'I was the ten-year-old watching *Today Tonight*,' he recalls, referring to the forerunner of RTÉ's modern-day *Prime Time*. The family simply followed the news, and the events of the day, more keenly than others. 'I'd be watching *Dempsey's Den* and my father would come in looking to switch over to the news. If you wanted to see *Home and Away*, you'd have to get out the portable TV.'

Griffin became more politically partisan by joining Young Fine Gael during his time studying in NUI Galway and made his first outing for the party on an unsuccessful attempt at a council seat in Dingle in the 2004 local elections. He recalls writing to Leo Varadkar, who had endured a similar defeat in 1999 but won the country's highest first-preference vote in 2004, and receiving a comprehensive email ('at some crazy hour of the night') encouraging him to remain optimistic and ambitious. (Varadkar, too, had had to work hard at building his reputation with his local electorate.) Reinvigorated, Griffin took on a role as Fine Gael's 'local area representative' – a manufactured title involving no public office, a 'fake it 'til you make it' pseudo-councillor role, as an elongated audition for the real thing – trying to drum up name recognition and potential voters.

The first attraction of public office, he says, was the notion that even small victories could have massive impact. As a member of a community group he would regularly go litter-picking, becoming recognisable to older parishioners. One approached him outside the local shop, wondering if someone could try to install a street-light outside the church, as it would often be worryingly dark after Saturday evening vigil Masses. 'And I'd organically say, "You know, I'll get onto the council about that and see what they do for me." And I'd end up writing letters as Joe Public, you know, and it would snowball from there.'

The letters would often go unanswered, which Griffin simply put down to being a random member of the public. 'You'd have to be a councillor, right? And you'd see the councillors' newsletters, and they'd claim to have done this, that and the other thing, and there am I, thinking, okay, the only way to get these things done is actually be in public office.'

The second motivation was anger: Griffin was running a pub in Castlemaine favoured by younger workers and could see takings sink week on week as more and more people fell out of work in the torrid years of 2009 and 2010. As a 28-year-old, he felt the anger of his generation more acutely than others, and channelled that frustration into the 2011 election bid. That energy carried Griffin to a somewhat unlikely win, unseating his party colleague Tom Sheahan in the three-seat constituency.

Griffin's story has parallels with that of Duncan Smith, a two-term Labour TD in Fingal. While his household was also one where the news was closely followed, there was no history of party political action. He was in the process of completing a doctorate at DCU, working in a call centre at weekends for a few extra quid, and he had just bought a house in Swords with his now-wife. A month later, the fall of the American financial services company Lehman Brothers prompted an international economic collapse.

'I just felt so vulnerable and angry. I felt that right at the moment where you feel that life is going to have a lot of possibilities, and you've done everything – you've done your school, you've gone to your college, you've got your work, you're developing your careers – and the rug is pulled out, and within months, you had massive job losses. Loads of my friends emigrated. The whole shebang.'

The resulting cutbacks also meant fewer roles in academia so that, even had Smith completed his doctorate, there would have been little prospect of being able to pursue a career as a lecturer.

'So I was really angry. And then, my dad said, "Look, why don't you just want to actually join a political party?" He literally said it like, "Don't be on the barstool or at the kitchen table talking about it at home. Go and do something."'

Becoming involved in the residents' association saw him introduced to then-senator Brendan Ryan, who was impressed with both Smith's passion and his organisational capability. Ryan invited Smith to run his general election campaign in Dublin North, an offer Smith was happy to accept. As it had become obvious that cutbacks would hamper his original plan of a career in academia, Smith then became Ryan's parliamentary assistant in Leinster House.

It is only with the benefit of hindsight that Smith is able to see how politically interested he had always been, without ever thinking of channelling it into a full-time pursuit. 'I was always involved in the Glencree Centre for Peace and Reconciliation, or part of cultural exchanges, and debating and stuff. A friend of mine put it through that I was probably always preparing for the job, and for public service, without actually realising I was doing it. Once I got involved, I felt that this is where I was meant to be.'

Smith pauses. 'That sounds massively corny.'

Leinster House might have been where Smith was meant to be, but electoral success was still something that had to be cultivated.

Ω

Tales like this are common. A householder needs help sorting out a medical appointment, or a social welfare payment, and is helped by a kind TD who then recruits them as a party supporter. A house burns down, and the local councillor helps the unfortunate family to get back on their feet. A senator shows up at a college debate and says something that lights a spark in an impressionable student. A bright new graduate is self-aware enough to realise how their education opened doors for them and wants to share that opportunity with others. A would-be taoiseach with an autistic sibling starts agitating local representatives for better services and ends up taking on the fight themselves.

Sometimes the ideals are plain. Louise O'Reilly of Sinn Féin was born a Dubliner and developed an interest in industrial relations partly because of her father's own trade unionism, and her mother having to give up her pensionable job in the Revenue Commissioners due to the 'marriage bar' that forbade married women from working in the public service. The loss of that job, O'Reilly says, stimulated her mother's interest in making sure her two daughters always made financial provision for their futures. But while many in the trade union movement would have gravitated to the Labour Party – and O'Reilly's own father was a longtime appointee to Labour's administrative council, though he never actually joined the party officially – O'Reilly's political outlook was more immediately sculpted by the 10 years of her childhood spent living in Dundalk.

'My mother would say I was a republican from the age of five. We'd be going over the border, and I'd be like, "It doesn't make any sense!" My mam had a sterling purse and a punt purse, and we would have gone swimming in Newry on a Saturday morning. So even as we were kids, I grew up a republican.'

ß

And sometimes, elsewhere close to the border, politics just falls into someone's lap: rather than someone spending years running for office and eventually pushing their way in, the profession finds a way of pulling in new blood.

The end of the 'dual mandate' from 2004, which meant TDs could no longer also hold seats on their county or city councils, created dozens of vacancies in 2003. Many full-timers in Leinster

House were giving up seats on local authorities and allowing their replacements to learn the ropes before contesting the 2004 local elections themselves. One such TD was Fine Gael's Seymour Crawford, who had to leave his spot on Monaghan County Council. Among the party's local membership there was nobody appropriate or available to be co-opted to the vacancy. One outsider suggested was Bert Stewart, a well-known figure in the local branch of the Irish Farmers' Association. Another was Bert's sister, the local credit union manager Heather Humphreys.

Crawford went to visit both, and reached a fork in the road in approaching the two houses. His chaperone directing him said: 'Left for Bert, right for Heather.' In Humphreys' retelling of the story, Crawford remarked, 'Oh, they're looking for women, I'll try her first.'

'He came to me, and he explained to me what it was, and he said, "I need to know tomorrow, by two o'clock. There's a convention on, and the nominations are closing." I had to go to my employers and ask them, was that okay? And in fairness, the credit union [staff] were all volunteers themselves, so they didn't mind.'

So began Humphreys' political career: being drafted in as a formal member of a party for whom she was already sympathetic, she contested the convention, and took Crawford's seat for the remainder of that term. 'I remember at first, starting to think, "Oh my goodness, what have you got yourself into?"

'But I always said, "Look, I'm getting an opportunity here to do something to make a difference. What right have I to stand up and give out about everybody, if I don't take this chance? This is an actual chance for me to do something, and make a difference in decision-making at local level." So I did it.'

Eleven years after that fateful fork in the road, Humphreys had found her way into cabinet. Someone who hadn't been a member of a political party was now a member of the Government of Ireland.

'The credit union was a great grounding for any kind of politics, because you're dealing with people,' she says. 'You're dealing with real people, real problems, and trying to sort out issues for them. You could give them the money they needed to get them out of some difficulty, or help them do something – maybe buy a car to get them to work – or loads of little things. You always felt you were making a difference to them.'

It was no harm that before the credit union, she had worked in more traditional retail banking for Ulster Bank, where she had received formal training on dealing with difficult customers. No matter what a politician's party affiliation or loyalty, there will always be a fair share of difficult customers to deal with.

2

ON THE TICKET

It is a big night in a bustling hotel. A general election is on the way, and party members are gathering for the constituency convention. Tonight, they will choose who goes forward to contest the general election for their party.

There is The Favourite: the local standard-bearer has already come close to landing a seat in Dáil Éireann, and though they haven't gotten over the line in their previous attempts, there is a sense that they are the locale's hardest worker, strongest candidate, and prospect with the greatest name recognition.

There is also The Challenger, but this challenger is neither terribly well known nor loved. They are respected, but not seen as a serious opponent to the frontrunner. They are unlikely to get the nod this time around, but nonetheless will put up a good show, planting a flag and strengthening a claim to be given another tilt in the years to come.

Piquing the interest of the local diehards as they file into the hotel is the presence of some relative strangers. Some people have shown up to the convention who have never darkened the door of a party event before. None of the top brass appear to know who these people are, and these strangers keep largely to themselves. This is curious, but not a major point of concern: as in most major parties, people may only vote at a convention if they have been paid-up members of the local branch for a few consecutive years. It is a level of pragmatic entryism: the principle of the rule is that nobody should be allowed to just show up and vote unless they have proven some commitment to the party. The presence of these strangers is therefore not seen as significant or in any way germane.

This is exactly how The Challenger wants it. The Favourite doesn't know it, but they have sleepwalked into an ambush.

The Strangers might never have attended a meeting before, but that doesn't mean they aren't long-standing members. Quietly, The Challenger has signed up legions of new members to the party branch – in cahoots with the party official who looks after the membership logs, who is also a supporter of The Challenger. Their presence in the books has been kept as a watertight secret until the moment of truth.

Not only that, but The Strangers are fully paid-up members too. They haven't even paid their membership fees out of their own pockets: some of The Challenger's other supporters have adopted the role of *de facto* benefactors, and have covered the membership fee on behalf of these fleeting visitors. But none of this matters: they're on the membership roll, their fees have been paid, and there's no way to stop them from voting. The Strangers have little interest in the politics of this or any party and are merely repaying previous favours to various other supporters of The Challenger.

The stealthy masterplan has come to fruition. When the time comes and the vote is called, they dutifully raise their hands, back The Challenger, and slip back into the night. No speeches are needed, no explanations are offered. They have done what they came to do: to audaciously sweep the convention in favour of The Challenger. And nobody – least of all The Favourite, who is stunned into seething silence – saw it coming.

After all, the first rule of politics is irrefutable: learn to count.

♟

This is a true story: the identities of those involved have been obscured only because nobody involved will speak on the record. Political anoraks and Leinster House habitués may be able to figure out who The Challenger is; however, they may not, because it's possible that the same strategy has been pursued by plenty of others. Depending on one's view, this is not a bug in the system, but rather a feature: if decisions are made by those who show up, simply make sure you produce enough eligible voters.

There is a golden rule of party conventions: if a candidate is unsure of their prospects, they are going to lose. Nobody should enter a room pinning their chances on blind hope, unable to predict how many votes will fall their way. Politics is a ruthless business: if you don't lock down a vote, someone else will – and a candidate who can't lock down the support of their own party colleagues will be seen as a pushover when it comes to knocking on doors and winning the support of total strangers.

A crowded field of candidates is good for a party looking to portray vibrance and vigour: a general election convention where three or four councillors want to run for the Dáil, and then all agree to get behind the singular winner, is a healthy process for an energised party. But not every field is crowded: sometimes it's three candidates running for two spots on the ballot paper, or two looking for one, raising the prospect of the branch being left divided and unable to reconcile itself with the outcome.

Sometimes this can be overcome by quiet whispers of assurance to the loser: don't worry, headquarters will wait a few months and then add you to the ticket anyway – the winner wins and gets a head start on the formal campaign, but the loser doesn't really lose. On other occasions the advice is more blunt: pull out now and save everyone the embarrassment of a fight you can't win. Make the party look good, and your time might come later. Makes us look bad and you're dead to us.

Contested conventions, one senator quips, are 'a hoor of a thing' to manage. The best-case scenario is that the loser performs well enough so as not to discredit themselves, but not so well as to inflict damage on the winner. A tricky situation to manage – and one which parties will often try to centrally control – is a race where the nominees include an incumbent TD (or, even worse, a sitting minister). In most cases, the incumbent should remain popular enough within their own organisation to sail through unimpeded. But there are occasions when a minister is not the flavour of the month with their party colleagues, and when other members – especially those whose own rise through the ranks was stalled by the presence of a newcomer – could pose a real danger. Running both candidates, simply to avoid a contested convention, might merely defer the same split in the ranks and project it onto a national stage. Worst-case scenario, you could have both candidates marginally short of election.

'There is always leakage,' says the senator. 'People think you'll always get the same percentage of the vote. You don't. Your extra candidate from the north might pick up a few more votes, but they just don't transfer fully back.'

This is a reference to Ireland's electoral system, where voters rank candidates in the order of their preference. In traditional thinking, a voter who gives their first preference to a candidate from a specific party might give their second preference to another candidate from the same fold. Once a candidate is assured of election, any surplus votes are redistributed to the candidates who received the number two votes on those ballot papers, and so on. If the preferred candidate is eliminated, every single ballot paper carrying their name is redistributed to the candidate with the next-highest preference beside their name.

The problem identified by the senator is that not every voter who backs the new candidate will give the second-preference vote to their established running mate. 'The candidate from the south might be depending on the same votes that the fella in the north has just got, and which don't transfer back. And if the fella from the south was running by himself, he would have got most of them anyway.'

A more exotic prospect arises when the convention has been told to choose only one candidate, and the sitting TD is not guaranteed of victory. This is a scenario riven with danger for all concerned. Defeat the TD, and that deputy becomes a lame duck for the rest of the term, demoralised and probably furious. Defeat a sitting minister, and the entire government is destabilised: how can someone contend to help run the country when even their own party wants rid of them? The pressure on The Challenger to pull out and save the blushes of the government as a whole can be immense. There may be promises of favouritism when it comes to choosing preferred candidates for the Seanad election that will follow the general. Such promises are not always easily delivered.

Irrespective of how the convention may go, or how many candidates might be featured in an optimal strategy, there is always a possibility of a last-minute addition. The introduction of gender quotas meant that for the 2016 and 2020 elections, parties would risk the loss of state funding if fewer than 30 per cent of their candidates nationwide were female. From 2024, that quota rose to 40 per cent. Given the bias at conventions towards sticking with incumbent TDs, parties are often left parachuting additional female candidates into some constituencies – an act which might redress a national imbalance but create a local one. Some last-minute candidates are at least self-aware enough to appreciate their fate, recognising they are there as geographical sweepers, gaining a few votes that might transfer to their better-established running mates. Others are less analytical and will throw themselves into a campaign hoping to maximise their own vote, both for the election at hand and for elections to come, irrespective of the cost to their stablemates.

An illustration of how much chicanery is involved in this comes from Dublin Bay South, a traditional Fine Gael heartland. That party was so aggrieved at the resignation of Lucinda Creighton in 2013 – and especially angered by her foundation of a brand-new party, Renua – that it went in hammer and tongs behind a new candidate, Kate O'Connell, who snatched the seat in 2016. O'Connell and her constituency colleague Eoghan Murphy were uneasy bedfellows, becoming particularly embittered during Fine Gael's leadership contest of 2017, when Murphy served as Leo Varadkar's campaign manager while O'Connell vocally supported his rival Simon Coveney.

The tide went out on Fine Gael in 2020, with O'Connell losing the seat and Murphy just about hanging on after a bruising period as minister for housing. However, the latter was so jaded from his stint in cabinet that he resigned his seat entirely only a year later. By then, O'Connell was so out of favour with Varadkar that she sat out the by-election, leaving James Geoghegan – more favoured by the party leader despite his own past association with Creighton and Renua – to run and finish second. Geoghegan was then selected to run in 2024, but rather than accept an olive branch from Simon Harris to rejoin the ticket, O'Connell announced to the *Sunday Independent* she would instead run as an independent. Fine Gael responded by pointedly adding another candidate of its own, Emma Blain, within hours of O'Connell's interview hitting the stands – all, ironically, to the apparent detriment of Geoghegan, who had publicly asked the party to stick to a one-candidate strategy in an effort to win back its long-held seat. Where Geoghegan had wanted to be the only candidate seeking support from Fine Gael-minded voters, now there were three. In the end, Geoghegan prevailed, and both women missed out.

ᛩ

The worst-case scenario might be where one contestant narrowly misses out, but is so determined to become a TD that they leave the party entirely. This is relatively common: Irish political history is littered with independent candidates who became electoral heavyweights simply because they were overlooked for candidacy within the party and decided to go it alone instead.

Every election features candidates who have fallen out of favour with headquarters, and who then pose problems on the double. Firstly, they split the vote: if the party has already judged that a one-candidate strategy is the best to maximise their hopes, the addition of a second like-minded candidate competing for the same votes is bad news electorally. Secondly, they split the organisation: if a critical mass of the local support follows the jilted candidate out the door, the remainder of the party can be left hollowed out, handicapped not just for the election at hand but for a generation to come.

The Healy-Rae dynasty in Kerry is perhaps the most famous example. Having directed 10 different contests – local elections, general elections, and even Dáil by-elections – for Fianna Fáil across the 1970s, '80s and '90s, as well as representing the party on Kerry County Council, Jackie Healy-Rae was overlooked to contest the 1997 general election for Kerry South. Initially expecting to be added to the ticket by party headquarters, he realised no such overture was forthcoming, so he called it quits. He ran under the unofficial banner of 'Independent Fianna Fáil', won – defeating one of the two Fianna Fáilers who had prevailed at the convention – and ended up becoming so integral to the next Dáil that his vote was crucial in ensuring the installation of a Fianna Fáil-led government, at the cost of exceptional investment in his southern bailiwick. Jackie's influence, demonstrably, ended up being much greater outside the party than within it. Nowadays, two of Jackie's sons are TDs – one of them a minister of state – and three of his grandchildren are county councillors, all of them poll-toppers, all of them running as independents. Fianna Fáil can only envy the electoral machine the family has become, and lament what was foregone by the failure to keep a savvy operator satisfied.

3

ON THE TRAIL

Most who have already come through a contested convention have proven their ability to manage their numbers, so the next step is to apply the same expertise to the electorate as a whole. For this, they need to milk a resource not commonly available to the public at large: the tallies.

Tallies are sometimes misunderstood by the public as a preliminary breed of election result. Rather, they are an unofficial calculation of the result, conducted by volunteers for political parties, entirely separately to the actual official counting of votes by returning officers and their teams. The tally – which merely entails standing over the ballot papers as they are removed from the ballot box, and taking notes of the first-preference candidate on each one – is conducted for two reasons. Firstly, it gives advance insight into the election outcome – is the candidate already destined for defeat? Should they bother attending the count themselves at all? Or is the candidate looking good, and can they start to think about preparing for office? After weeks of party members pounding pavements and begging for votes, with little tangible insight on how the race is going, early scraps of info are manna.

The second and more potent outcome is the extra insight that can be gleaned from the votes in each ballot box. Ahead of every election, the local returning officer will publish a 'polling scheme', listing the number of individual ballot boxes in the constituency, the polling stations those boxes will be based in, and the 'electoral divisions' that vote in each one. This allows knowledgeable candidates to identify exactly which boxes correspond with certain areas – and experienced insiders can quickly glean useful expertise about where their votes are literally coming from. All of the votes from one housing estate, for example, might all be in the same ballot box, and so a healthy return of first-preference votes illustrates that the residents there are happy with whatever it is the local candidate is offering.

This information is then recycled not just for the next election, but also for the time in between: if these voters are the ones who got you elected last time, it is only prudent to keep knocking on their doors and offering your services, so that they see you as a devoted representative when the next election comes. On a similar note, knowledge of previous tallies can identify scope for improvement: a candidate whose seat is on the line will not only double down on their existing voters, but tactically expand their operation to poach support from those who voted for similar opponents. Perhaps last time those voters gave the candidate their second preference; perhaps next time they might give them their number one.

This insight can be refined even further by bigger parties, if they have spare personnel on the day of elections to act as 'personation agents'. On the face of it, this allows parties and other registered interests to place someone in the polling station all day, taking note of those who present themselves to vote, and theoretically making sure that nobody receives a ballot paper under false pretences.

As an aside: this hasn't always been the case. Older campaigners will admit to canvassing at urban doors on the days of elections, taking note of houses with piles of unclaimed polling cards from former tenants, checking the register of electors and guessing which voters were no longer resident. A plucky party acolyte might then show up, claiming the abandoned identity and hoping to vote incognito. Some canvassers would even ask the resident if they could step into the front hall of the house, out of the wind or rain, and try to collect the disused polling cards in doing so. The personation agent at the station, if affiliated to the same party, would turn a blind eye and facilitate the very practice they were nominally there to prevent. Polling clerks now work in pairs for the entirety of polling day, from 7 a.m. to 10 p.m., as a human screen to prevent people showing up to vote multiple times using different identities, at least in the same ballot box.

The more practical reason personation agents are there is to ensure a party has its own record of exactly who showed up to vote. An estate with 200 homes could potentially have 500 or more registered voters, but a well-informed canvassing team can use these records to at least figure out which households did not vote at all, and therefore which ones were more likely to have yielded a vote for their candidate. Knocking on doors can be made more efficient as a result.

For much of the twentieth century, before housing estates became so plentiful and Ireland's population began rising so quickly, expert tallymen were so infinitely familiar with their local turf that it was sometimes possible to identify the swing voters almost by name. The three general elections held within an 18-month window across 1981 and 1982 yielded three successive sets of tallies for areas where the population was almost completely unchanged. Comparison of each tally, and analysis of the records of who actually voted, made it much more possible to find the crucial voter who had switched allegiance between Fianna Fáil and Fine Gael during the titanic battles of Charles Haughey and Garret FitzGerald. Armed with this granular insight, local party hacks could then look to engineer a chance social encounter between the swing voter and the local deputy, or a visiting minister, or even the taoiseach himself. One strategic handshake and a hospitable smile could be enough to turn the swing voter into a loyalist.

Although political parties tend to co-operate in compiling tallies at election counts, the actual data harvested is not commonly made public. At best, tally teams might now use live online spreadsheets, which can be copied and scrutinised later by a keen observer who knows where to look. But this art is so well refined by its practitioners, and so commonly underappreciated by political novices, that it gives established politicians a massive head start in an election campaign. Little buoys the heart of a politician scrambling for a seat more than the sight of a naïve challenger knocking on a door bidding for votes that are almost certainly not there to be won.

The most disciplined canvassing is less of a sociological study and more of a data-driven marketing campaign. In its heyday, Fianna Fáil's ultimate calling card was its ability to marshal enormous numbers of canvassers on urban streets on brighter summer evenings, taking meticulous note of the local concerns and quantifying the data at the end of the night. It is commonly believed that Bertie Ahern tended to stick with summer elections, and election canvassing during the brightest evenings of May and June, simply because his party was better at retail politics than anyone else.

Astute analysis of the data will yield important insights into the biggest issues, and the possible votes to be won by offering possible solutions. If there are enough bodies, there are also economies of scale – the candidate themselves might only spend a few seconds at each doorstep introducing themselves, while a volunteer then picks up the task of explaining their priorities. The candidate, more of a travelling salesman, can then be summoned to clinch any vote that appears to be up for grabs. Do this multiple times and a positive enough seed is planted that the candidate should become almost irresistible.

'The best analogy I've heard for canvassing is that it's the offline version of the very targeted ads you get online,' says one canvasser. 'You know how, if you go browsing for something like a soccer jersey, you then see ads for those jerseys everywhere you go? That's how the best canvassing should be – someone tells you their concern, and on a follow-up visit, you should be absolutely clinical about bringing it up again.'

For this reason, the best canvassing is often done in the months before an election. By the time the campaign has been called, especially in built-up urban areas of city constituencies, it may be common to bump into rival teams that are working the same street – and if canvassing is already seen as an inconvenience to the householder, woe betide the team that knocks on the door of a frazzled parent who has already been disrupted once in the middle of the children's dinner time. Those who are committed enough to do so, and have the resources and time to put in, find they are better served by meeting households well in advance of the starting gun being formally fired. Gary Gannon has found that in the post-Covid era, Friday afternoons can be an excellent time to knock on doors: there's likely to be a higher proportion of people working from home, but their concentration on work is waning and they're likely to welcome some respite – even if it's a politician checking in on them or trying to butter them up for a vote.

Advance canvassing also allows for the possibility of some freelance fixing, a sort of dress rehearsal for the part of an elected politician. One seasoned politician tells newcomers, especially those running for the council, to ask householders what they'd like sorted and to try to do it even before getting into the job. Most level-headed voters might merely expect the candidate to promise action if and when they actually get the job – 'vote for me and I'll sort it out'. More enterprising candidates are encouraged to go a step further, ringing up the county council in the guise of a local resident, voicing the concern and suggesting a possible solution.

They might then be able to go back to the same household, closer to the time of the election, and tell them conclusively that they have already got the ball rolling on addressing the big problem.

For those struggling to understand that suggestion, the veteran even offers a template for a canvasser's conversation:

'"Hello there, sorry to bother you. My name is Blank and I'm going to be a candidate in the general election in a few months. Do you have a minute to talk?"

'"Yes, nice to meet you. Jaysus, you're out early …"

'"Ah, you know yourself, no harm in trying to get a head start! Every vote is going to count! Can I ask what you are finding as the biggest issues for you at the minute?"

'"Actually, to be honest, the biggest one I can think of at the minute is the traffic locally. Since they finished the new estate up the road, there is loads more traffic trying to get onto the main road and it's difficult to get out of here."

'Then you go to the next house. Same routine. "What are you finding as the biggest issues?"

'"Oh, the cost of childcare. It's outrageous. It took us ages to find a crèche for our twins and the cost of it is higher than the mortgage."

'This is a harder issue to tackle because, as merely an aspiring TD, you can't promise to sort it. The best thing you can do is try to talk about what your national spokesperson is doing on that issue, and if you're an independent you can't even do that.

'So you give a holding response: "I completely agree, it's definitely an enormous issue, and I promise to fight tooth and nail for more spaces and more subsidies if I'm elected. By any chance, how are you finding the traffic around here at morning time?"

'"Oh, it's poxy. Absolutely cat. It's backed up all the way to the middle of the estate now, since the new development opened."

'So you go away and ring the council, and ask how best to make an approach to the county engineer. You tell them that traffic is building up at this junction, and that maybe they should consider installing traffic lights, or putting a yellow box on the road, so that the people in the estate still have a way of cutting through the traffic. You could try to pull a fast one and use the language that suggests you're actually a resident.

'But if you have any luck getting hold of the right people, then you have an ace up your sleeve for the next time you are canvassing, probably closer to election time. "Hello again! I don't know if you remember, I was here talking to you a few months ago about running for the election – you mentioned you were having serious trouble with the traffic here in the estate? I have brought it to the county engineer who says he is looking at the feasibility of putting in traffic lights, so that there might be a gap in the traffic for you to still get out during the morning commute."

'"Really? Oh, God, that would be great. It's getting so hard to have the twins in the crèche on time, that would be a huge help. Super stuff!"

'"Well, glad I could be of service – I will leave you with my flyer, I would really appreciate your vote."

'"No bother at all, fair play to you, great stuff."

'Mission accomplished,' the veteran concludes, smiling at the thought of a vote well won.

The result of the 2020 election, with three parties winning roughly equal numbers of seats, meant that the resulting Dáil had very few constituencies with two incumbents from the same party. Consequently the election of 2024 had precious few examples of running mates fighting tooth and nail against each other for the final seats in their shared constituencies. But little sets hair flying more than the internecine war between two candidates on the same ticket, who believe that only one has any prospect of squeezing in.

'It was the first time I ever heard the phrase "piss and vinegar",' says one former TD who has seen two constituency colleagues taking lumps out of each other. 'And I've never heard a phrase more appropriate. They are brutal.'

Such contests can easily arise. With constituencies being designed as they are, with county boundaries given primacy in how the borders are drawn up, it's almost always the case that a constituency will have multiple large towns or conurbations. Elections in Louth always have the subplot of amounting to internal races around Dundalk and Drogheda. The election then becomes an arms race: if any party runs candidates from either town, so must everyone else, even if only one can win.

But which one? Both candidates will hope to be the last one standing, outpolling the other so that when the lower finisher is eliminated, the lion's share of their votes will transfer to their party colleague and propel them back to Leinster House. It might take an extraordinary turn of events to see both winning. Hence, the rivalry between them can be equally extraordinary in scale.

This animosity can sometimes be overblown, one party official believes, given some constituencies incorporate two full counties. In these examples (like Cavan–Monaghan or Carlow–Kilkenny) there is little or no reason for candidates to cross the county boundary because voters will always prefer their local candidate. But, the same official acknowledges, in physically smaller constituencies the contest can be especially vicious. 'When you are running against another party the priorities are straightforward – make sure you get as much media exposure as possible, the best locations for your election posters, that sort of thing. But if you have more than one candidate, you have party headquarters trying to decide which one takes up an invitation for a radio debate, and even if you try to spread the opportunities, one of them will end up pissed off.'

It is rare that such an election goes by where two running mates don't fall into dispute about the internal partitioning of the constituency. Headquarters may draw a line across a tactical divide, splitting the constituency in the mould of King Solomon. This is ostensibly intended to make sure each candidate has the opportunity to maximise their own first-preference vote, but inevitably results in more grievances about the territory allocated, and paranoia in each candidate that HQ is stifling them in favour of the other. Even when the dividing line is grudgingly accepted, there will often be disputes about sightings of one candidate's canvass team or 'vote number 1' posters inside the territory allotted to the other. Policing the placing of posters is becoming harder in some areas: candidates in constituencies bordering Dublin or Cork cities will sometimes place posters along the main commuter roads to draw the attention of bored motorists. If it's okay to place a poster for a candidate in (say) Meath East on the M3 in Dublin West, it's harder to take issue with a poster being in the 'wrong' end of the correct constituency.

The most infamous example of intra-party warfare came in 2007, when Bertie Ahern was leading the charge for a third term in office. Fianna Fáil already held two seats of the three in Dublin Central, but a fourth was being added and Ahern was determined to reinforce his control. The party decided that a three-candidate strategy was its best bet, seeking to maximise geographical spread across the expanded constituency. Ahern was joined on the ticket by Mary Fitzpatrick, daughter of his retiring running mate Dermot, and Cyprian Brady, who had run his constituency office. Sensing that Ahern would have more than enough first-preference votes of his own, Fitzpatrick circulated a flyer on the night before polling inviting would-be Bertie supporters to lend her their first-preference votes instead. Furious at this perceived slight on the incumbent taoiseach, Ahern's team delivered 30,000 leaflets on the morning of the vote, explicitly asking Bertie voters to stick with him for their first-preference votes, and to give their second preferences to Brady. Fitzpatrick, in this scenario, would be the third preference.

Fitzpatrick's original assessment was vindicated when the votes were counted: Fianna Fáil had won 44 per cent of the vote, more than enough to secure two of the four seats, but Ahern had taken 37 per cent of it all by himself. With only 20 per cent needed for the 'quota' that guarantees a seat, the surplus 17 per cent was distributed … and benefited Brady over Fitzpatrick by a ratio of two to one. Out of almost 35,000 votes cast, Brady had won only 939 first-preference votes out of almost 35,000, but leapfrogged Fitzpatrick thanks to the handsome surplus votes of his party leader. Fitzpatrick's own eventual elimination resulted in the remaining Fianna Fáil vote snowballing to Brady and ensuring his eventual success. Only one TD in history had ever been elected with fewer first preferences.

Fitzpatrick would accuse Ahern of shafting her; Ahern's stalwarts responded that she had fired the first shot by trying to claim some of the taoiseach's enormous personal vote for herself. Their grievance may have been legitimate, but the excuse was imperfect: Ahern's leaflet was so professionally designed and extensively circulated that it was unlikely to have been a last-minute idea. Nonetheless, Brady got his term in Dáil Éireann; Fitzpatrick ran in four subsequent elections but has yet to make it as a TD.

Examples of collegial running mates are so rare as to almost be immediately identifiable. One is the pair of Sinn Féin TDs in Dublin Mid-West, Eoin Ó Broin and Mark Ward. Ward entered the Dáil in November 2019 in a by-election, to fill the seat left behind by MEP Frances Fitzgerald. Sinn Féin's victory on the day was somewhat unexpected, and a harbinger for the party's success in the general election to come – but the challenge was then how to retain both seats in a competitive four-seater when the general election followed, three months later. The best solution, Ó Broin found, was to go one step further than merely dividing up the constituency between them: it was actually knocking on doors as a duo, and having one candidate ask voters, to their faces, to give their first-preference vote to the other.

The system worked: buoyed by the overall rise of the Sinn Féin tide nationwide, the party confounded conventional expectations to retain both seats. So well managed was their vote that it even benefited others: People Before Profit's Gino Kenny retained the final seat, in no small part because of how expertly Sinn Féin had corralled its own supporters, with Ó Broin having a healthy surplus that not only sealed Ward's seat but left enough of a spillover to help other left-wing candidates too.

ȣ

Innocent candidates can often think that by polling day, there is simply nothing else to be done. When the votes have been cast, what more can we do? This is, in fairness, mostly true: naturally, once the public has voted there is scant more that can be done to influence the race – except, where the circumstances permit, to challenge the validity of the occasional ballot.

As votes are processed and sorted in count centres, disputes will occasionally be raised about the provenance of some ballots. Some will be missing the official stamp from the returning officer. This is almost always a simple clerical oversight, a polling clerk forgetting to put the imprint onto the ballot, which unfortunately renders that vote null.

Then there are ballot papers which have an additional message from the voter – some kind of slogan or political view expressed instead of, or in addition to, the numbers beside each candidate's name. These also result in a vote being considered as spoiled: distinguishable handwriting of any sort on a ballot paper is considered sufficient to make the voter identifiable, no matter how unlikely that is in practice, and for the overall secrecy of the ballot to be compromised.

Campaign teams will occasionally challenge this principle anyway: in 2019 there were 12 candidates contesting the local elections in Ballyfermot–Drimnagh, leaving 12 boxes in which voters would express their preferences for each candidate. One voter, presumably not native to Ballyfermot, used those 12 boxes to write the message 'M-A-Y-O-4-S-A-M-2-0-1-9'. This prompted some admittedly brief discussion as to whether the vote should be declared valid, as one candidate had the figure '1' – from '2-0-1-9' – inscribed beside their name. This argument was, eventually, as successful as Mayo's challenge for Sam Maguire that year: the westerners lost to Dublin in the All-Ireland semi-final. (A similar challenge arose in the UK, which uses a non-numerical 'first past the post' system, where a voter described every candidate on their ballot as 'wank', with the exception of one candidate, whose box was inscribed with the words 'not wank'. The campaign team of that candidate claimed, eventually unsuccessfully, that this should be considered as a legitimate indication of preference.)

Another more unusual form of spoiled vote is where the voter has placed a number beside the name of each candidate, and did not include any messages or other unacceptable inscriptions … but failed to include a number one. This is more common than many would appreciate: on days where voters are handed two or more ballot papers, like when local and European elections occur on the same day, some electors will treat the two distinct ballot papers, for two distinct elections, as if they were a single entity. If there were 10 candidates on one ballot paper, and 10 on another, they might write numbers 1 through 20 across the two papers. This previously resulted in inconsistent approaches, depending on the view of the returning officer: if a list of numbers starts without a 1, is it void immediately? Or could it be accepted because the voter had still illustrated an order of preference for which candidates they preferred? Sometimes it even depended on whether the numbers on the page were in an unbroken sequence, so numbers 2-5-6-8 might be unacceptable, but numbers 5-6-7-8 could pass the test. Only after a contentious count in Listowel,

County Kerry, in 2014 was the matter referred to the courts. The Supreme Court clarified that if a ballot paper was to be filled out numerically, a paper without a number one did not meet the legal requirements to be counted.

There are differing views in politics about whether this ruling was the correct one – and different views about whether the government should have introduced fresh laws to reintroduce some leeway where a voter has, in all probability, expressed a clear order of preference. Supporters of Sinn Féin and other left-leaning parties believe successive governments opted against undoing the ruling because it was more likely to affect voters from working-class areas, which often have lower levels of civic education, and where establishment parties might win fewer votes anyway. Figures in Fianna Fáil and Fine Gael counter that the error is just as common among older voters, who were lifelong supporters of one or other party, and who have been voting in this procedurally incorrect manner for their whole lives without anyone ever having cause to tell them not to.

In any event, it is common for the largest parties to have a few legal eagles hovering around centres to weigh in on the acceptability and provenance of any contested ballot papers. Most returning officers are assertive enough to reach their own conclusions, but having a self-assured barrister nearby to weigh in for a candidate can't do any harm.

4

FINDING YOUR FEET

'Hogwarts,' says one TD, when asked for their first impressions of working life in Leinster House. 'Hogwarts, except with a Celtic Tiger-era multistorey extension.'

This TD had not been a member of a local authority before finding themselves catapulted into the heart of Irish democracy. For them the learning curve was slightly steeper: not having been a councillor meant having to get to grips with the sometimes arcane nature of parliamentary procedures, as well as the cast of characters pulling the strings behind the scenes. But even for those with long political careers behind them, and who are comfortable with the protocols of engagement, Leinster House can still be a tough place to settle into.

Another offers a parallel to the Hogwarts analogy: 'I describe Leinster House as having the stuffiness of a golf club, and the faux intrigue of *Gossip Girl*.'

Those who are elected with enormous mandates and promises to fight like hell for their downtrodden constituents, often take weeks – if not months – to truly find their feet. Elections are high profile, but the practice of politics is often discreet and tedious, especially for those who make constituency cases their bread and butter.

Imagine yourself newly elected as a TD and being contacted by a pensioner complaining about the waiting list for their hip replacement. You promise to help them, and to at least make a case for their surgery being expedited, but once you hang up the phone, what exactly do you do? You can't just ring up the minister for health to complain (you probably don't have their number anyway) – and even if you did, they would merely tell you they can't interfere and that you should ring the HSE, who might take weeks to get back to you with even a noncommittal holding reply. Nor can you ring up the hospital where you expect the surgery would be carried out. But try telling that to Bridie, who is in agony trying to get out of bed, who literally put herself in harm's way visiting the polling station to vote for you, who can't afford to wait for coalition talks to conclude so that a new minister for health can be appointed, and who will not be so understanding about the teething problems as you set up your offices in the constituency and in Leinster House.

The process of finding your place in the Oireachtas is sometimes literal. The original Georgian Leinster House is nowhere near large enough to house offices for all deputies and their staff, and now the only TD with an office inside the eighteenth-century building is the Ceann Comhairle. Everyone else is farmed out to offices in the two multistorey buildings adjoining the complex, which are usually assigned on the basis of party strength. Some independent TDs are technically off the campus entirely, in the nearby headquarters of the Department of Agriculture. In general, what these TDs sacrifice in proximity they make up for in space; their offices have a much larger footprint than those in the main campus.

But the layout of the campus and the underground tunnels that connect some of the buildings is not always intuitive. One prominent TD revealed that it took three years for them to realise that there was an underground tunnel connecting Leinster House proper to the LH2000 extension that houses the committee rooms. They simply presumed that everyone else, like them, was sprinting through the winds and occasional downpours trying to get from one speaking slot to another. Those with offices in separate buildings on the campus have an extra challenge: getting to the chamber within eight minutes when the Dáil bells are ringing to summon members for a vote. For the unfamiliar, it can be quite a sprint. The doors to the chamber are locked after eight minutes, with no way in or out; this includes the door to the Press Gallery, after a tardy TD climbed over the ledge of the press seating and into the chamber to participate.

Staffing those offices is perhaps the first great challenge. Every TD is entitled to one parliamentary assistant and one administrative assistant, both on the payroll of the Oireachtas but answerable directly to the politician. Mindful of how exhausting and thankless the hours may be, a large number of politicians give these jobs to immediate family members. This is why, in the early months of a new Dáil, it is common to see critical press coverage about how many politicians have given cushy jobs to their spouses or children. Brendan Griffin gave the two jobs to his cousin Tommy and his wife, Róisín. To him, there was never any doubt that they were the best hires: 'They were the two people who were there with me, handing out leaflets outside churches. Doing all these things, well in advance of when I was running for the Dáil in 2011. So it was no question for me, this would be the team I'd be keeping together.' Ironically, he felt, the Dublin-based media had made more of an issue of his appointments than the media in his native Kerry. The dynastic element of Kerry politics, with the Healy-Rae family long presenting close family ties as providing more efficient public service, made the idea of recruiting relatives much more tolerable.

A more generous explanation is that the hours of an assistant will regularly match the crazy hours the politician themselves must work, and a purely employer–employee relationship may be ill-suited to the gruelling and emotive nature of the job. Plus, though the workplace is glamorous, the work isn't – and often entails getting an earful from a constituent with an axe to grind. Nor is the money particularly great, but more about that later.

The other approach is to find staff who share your political ideology and outlook, and who have previous experience in a similar role. For those without experience in public office, this is even more crucial: a wise advisor will help the newbie to discern the difference between the Dáil Business Committee and the Select Dáil Committee on Business. (Yes, there is a difference: the first discusses the Dáil's agenda for the coming days; the second scrutinises legislation proposed by the minister for enterprise.)

Some parties actively try to help newcomers over the hump of the job by helping to arrange the staffing. Sinn Féin is said to be particularly sensitive to the inexperience of some new TDs, and tries to assign some of the more experienced staff to its novice deputies. There are differing views on whether this is an attempt to 'get the measure' of new politicians, and even for the party to keep a central eye on its members.

Louise O'Reilly of Sinn Féin says the truth is somewhere in between: that deputies can ask the party to take care of appointments centrally, merely because it has better institutional knowledge of the qualities needed for a good staff member. For the first year and a half, her parliamentary assistant was Kathryn Reilly, who had previous experience working for Louth TD Arthur Morgan before herself becoming a one-term member of the Seanad. Having an assistant with experience of public representation themselves was 'incredibly helpful' in getting O'Reilly up to pace with parliamentary rhythms. (That said, O'Reilly found it easier than most to do so: given a previous career in industrial relations, being party to marathon talks yielding the likes of wage agreements, she describes herself as a 'procedure wonk'.) An even bigger asset, O'Reilly believes, is her administrative assistant, Marian Buckley. 'If there was a transfer window, there isn't a TD in Dáil Éireann who wouldn't vote for Marian.' Marian herself became so taken with the idea of public representation that she ran for Fingal County Council in 2024.

A more practical reason for asking a party to take central control over staff appointments is to save the deputy from having to turn down their local applicants. Others outside Sinn Féin can see the benefit of this model: a well-meaning local who fails to get the job might quickly become a thorn in the side with an axe to grind, and nobody wants to give the benefit of the doubt to someone local but then find that they're not quite cut out for the hours.

🔑

Some parts of learning the ropes are better managed than others. The HR side of things is now well managed by the Oireachtas: new members show up at a 'one-stop shop' and are presented with forms for having their salaries and allowances paid, getting set up on internal email systems and issued with work devices, even signing direct debit forms so that unpaid restaurant and bar tabs can be deducted from their salaries. The last point has only become necessary in more recent years: an honour system previously prevailed where somebody could add their lunch to a tab and eventually be trusted to show up and clear off the arrears, but some politicians got into bad habits about paying, and a few even left their parliamentary careers behind without having fully paid for their food and drink on the premises.

But as regards learning to do the job of a TD? There is no manual, and nobody to hold your hand. From the political perspective, the only help given is in two documents. 'You're handed a copy of the Standing Orders,' says one TD – referring to the internal rules of the Dáil and Seanad, which govern exactly how the two chambers conduct their affairs – 'and a copy of the constitution. And that's it. That's your full briefing.'

One TD elected in 2011, at a time of unusual churn and a large number of novices, felt thrown in at the deep end and only learned the basics of parliamentary life through nuggets picked up from other beginners. 'I looked up at the monitor one day and saw one of the other newbies speaking in the chamber,' they confide. 'As soon as they had finished, I went into the chamber myself, sat beside them, and asked how they had managed to get a speaking slot. It was only then that I learned about having to book one with a party whip.'

One TD admits to a mortifying mix-up after finally plucking up the courage to nab themselves a speaking slot. 'The only debating I'd ever seen was in college debating societies where maiden speakers were given this special treatment, wrapped up in cotton wool – so I thought I'd be treated with kid gloves and given a few token minutes to thank my constituents and throw out some rough ideas for the things I wanted to tackle.'

It was only about thirty seconds before being called that this deputy realised there were no such airs and graces in Dáil Éireann, and their debut speech would be in the middle of a fully fledged debate on government legislation. 'I had to abandon about two-thirds of what I had planned to say, and speak on the hoof about an area I hadn't any particular interest in. I think I was down [to speak] for five minutes, but sat down again after two. I just sat on my hands in the chamber for the next twenty minutes, afraid to look at my phone in case I had been found out for spoofing in my first ever speech.'

If that deputy felt mortified at speaking on the hoof, it is unlikely they remained so nervous a speaker for so long. 'There was a time in my life when the thought of going on *Drivetime* and being grilled by Sarah McInerney would have left me with cold shivers,' says Gary Gannon of the Social Democrats, 'whereas now, give me twenty minutes' notice, and I can probably go on and [give] a good account of whatever the topic is I'm going to be talking about. That comes from a bit of experience, a little bit more confidence, and also the fact that I've had to do it over the course of the last four years when I've had many different things I've had to speak on.'

Another former novice was in their office, trying to get to grips with the extensive new paperwork, when a chime started playing over the public address system. Slightly baffled – not having been told to expect any votes that morning – the deputy poked a head out of their office door, but saw no colleagues nearby to offer any guidance. Hurriedly, presuming an unscheduled vote had been called, this deputy grabbed a necktie and suit jacket and hastily blundered down to the chamber within the eight allotted minutes before the doors were to be sealed. It was only when they got to the door of the chamber, and saw the benches in their usual state of near-abandonment, that they realised the chime was not the one they had previously heard when deputies were summoned for votes. What they had heard was not the Dáil division bell, but rather the chime signalling the start of business in the Seanad. 'There just wasn't anybody to tell you these things,' that TD still laments, grateful that they hadn't injured themselves in their haste to make it down a few flights of stairs.

☋

In the first few months, before the machinery of a new government gets into full gear and Oireachtas committees are formed to give extra structure to their working day, members can almost find themselves idle. Some, hoping to remain (literally) visible while they find their feet, will sit in the Dáil chamber – not with the intention of speaking, but simply to observe and feel like participants in the affairs of the nation. Many will tuck into the seats behind their party leader so that, when the leader inevitably speaks at Leaders' Questions or in the daily discussion on 'promised legislation', they can hope to appear on national television and, by extension, maybe the TV news bulletins. Ministers are on a rota to appear alongside the taoiseach or tánaiste on the government benches; opposition parties usually whip some of their deputies to do likewise whenever their leader has a speaking opportunity.

What those new TDs inevitably learn is that the race to appear on TV is futile – unless they breach decorum and get involved in a cross-floor slagging match, speaking out of turn and risking some token admonition from the Ceann Comhairle, there is little scope to influence what makes the cut for the news. The quick realisation is that unless a TD has a speaking slot, sitting in the chamber is a fairly unproductive way of passing the time: it's time spent away from a computer or phone, where constituents' queries could be followed up.

One TD was leading a school tour from his constituency when he happened upon an accessible way to explain why the chamber was almost always empty. 'It's like a school timetable. If you imagine the chamber as a classroom, and you treat your interests or your portfolio like a subject, it begins to make more sense. If you're a TD whose main interest is English, you're not going to show up in the classroom when they're teaching maths.'

The same, media will point out, is true of themselves. Being absent from the chamber does not mean turning their back on proceedings; the ban on using laptops or iPads in the Press Gallery simply means that the hardest place to report on the Dáil is from the Dáil chamber itself.

ʔ

A challenge often faced by many as they find their feet is figuring out what kind of TD they think of themselves as being. Does the new deputy consider themselves to be a legislator? Are they a community fixer? Are they the parliamentary manifestation of a local cause or movement? Are they biding their time, trying to climb the professional ladder until they might command a ministry? Are they some or all of the above?

The larger parties in the Dáil tend to have some members from all of these categories. Some are wonks who like the chapter and verse of legislation and enjoy poring over its implications and interpretations. Some are known as having businesses in their locales – publicans, hoteliers, doctors, pharmacists – and garner reputations as community champions. Some come in on a single-issue matter like community healthcare or a contentious government policy. And some – many? most? – want power.

Even if they already know which style they want to pursue, finding the right balance between all of these aspects is a permanent challenge, and making the time to tend to all of those roles is a regular difficulty. Duncan Smith of Labour already knew the ropes from working for a former TD, but still had to figure out what *sort* of TD he wanted to be. 'What am I going to do similarly or the same, and what am I going to try and do differently? What can I do that's the same? What can't I do? That is quite idiosyncratic, but that's something I found a big adjustment.'

While Smith's instinct was to remain as close to the constituency as possible, family circumstances played their part. His son was born in December 2018; the new father had contested three elections – local, by-election and general – within his first 14 months. Certain times, like Sunday afternoons and evenings, had to be ringfenced as family time, even if that meant missing a half-dozen constituency events each week. Labour had a long history of running constituency clinics, which provided an important pipeline of work; but equally, for the youngest and newest Labour representative in the Dáil – a rare green shoot for a party which had undergone plenty of electoral turmoil – there was an expectation to be prominent on national media. Throw in his own desire to be a meaningful legislator, scrutinising the bills of others and tabling some of his own, and the challenge is neatly illustrated.

'It's always a balance, and I think one of the key things is you never feel like you're doing any one thing really, really well. If you're having a good couple of weeks on the constituency front, and you're on top of a couple of local issues – you're bringing your timetable changes to Irish Rail that are impacting thousands of people – then there's something else that's fallen behind. And then your personal responsibility shifts as well – maternity leaves ending; work schedules; crèche becomes ECCE becomes Junior Infants and afterschool and all that. So everything's shifting the whole time. It's always shifting.

'You never feel like you're getting that balance right. I don't think you can. I think you just have to accept, with this job, that there are so many competing pressures on us, and that you're never going to be on top of everything all the time.'

Noel Rock had a similar outlook. 'I see this clearer now that I'm out: you really could be a "busy fool",' he says, advocating the case for working smarter instead of harder. 'I think it's so important to keep the decks clear, maintain focus, and pursue "North Star" goals single-mindedly if you're going to get anywhere with them. Everyone wants your time and everyone wants to drag you in different directions. You need to be master and commander.'

⚷

Eventually the office will find itself operating with a full staffing complement, and constituency work will begin to come in. Bridie is still in need of her hip replacement; a middle-aged homebuyer thinks their property tax isn't being calculated correctly; a young dad has realised his daughter's passport may not be issued in time for the long-awaited holiday; an angry mother is fed up waiting for her son's assessment of need for a suspected intellectual disability. The work is varied and no two queries are ever quite the same.

An invaluable means of finding answers for those constituents comes in the form of a privilege that many of the public simultaneously expect, and yet are unaware of: the use of special hotlines run by most public bodies to handle queries exclusively from Oireachtas members. Some political parties – particularly the smaller ones, for whom resources are thin and continuity is key – will already have a list of these compiled so that an incoming TD has an immediate point of contact for a passport query or a tax complaint. Other parties don't have the culture of sharing these, and rookie deputies are left to flounder and sort out their own affairs, or at least to scrape together whatever details they can find from the offices of longer-serving colleagues.

A shortcut used by some resourceful newbies is to table a written parliamentary question to each member of cabinet, specifically asking them for the Oireachtas hotline of each agency under their remit. Best to do this early in the term, though: TDs' offices do keep an eye out for interesting questions being tabled by others, and a member who is visibly only compiling this list midway through the term is inadvertently highlighting their vulnerability to others. Several TDs noticed, for example, when one of their fellow parliamentarians went down this route in the summer of 2024, close to the end of that Dáil's natural lifetime. Some were baffled – 'What were they at for the last four years?' – while others took it as a visible admission of weakness: a TD looking for shortcuts in the summer before a general election is a TD who knows their seat is in jeopardy.

Dealing with these queries becomes the daily grind of a deputy's life, even if it isn't what they got into politics to do. Paul Murphy's propulsion into the Dáil in a high-profile by-election in 2014 – an electoral manifestation of the national movement against introducing water charges – meant he was not always expected to spend time on constituency casework. 'Given the moment, people looked to you not primarily as someone to get their street fixed, or whatever, but as someone who is going to build a movement against water charges and other injustices,' he says.

Finding his feet in Leinster House was perhaps a little easier for him than for most; it wasn't the start of a new Dáil term, and he was joining a Dáil grouping of six other TDs who, by his own light-hearted framing, 'weren't exactly jockeying for ministerial position' given their anti-capitalist position. Murphy had already had experience of being an MEP, having been co-opted to fill the seat of Joe Higgins when the veteran socialist leader returned to the Dáil in 2011. Higgins, under whom Murphy had first worked in Brussels, was now among his colleagues in Leinster House, helping to show him the ropes.

But over time, as water charges were seen off and the momentum from that single issue began to wane, the constituency casework began to come into his office instead. It's work he's happy to carry out – 'I think I'm a good constituency TD now, dealing with case work' – but it's work he doesn't believe a full-time national legislator should have to deal with.

A post-lockdown backlog in passport applications stands out to him as an exemplar of a broken system. Curtailments on international travel meant the staffing of the national passport office had been downsized, with staff seconded to other functions in the public service. The lifting of restrictions and the appetite for travel meant an immediate surge in people applying for new or renewed passports, with lengthy turnaround times, and many TDs receiving pleas from constituents whose holiday plans were at risk of falling victim to the backlog.

'People were going mad you couldn't get through to the passport office – and you know, we get queries about passports, we do our best – but then their answer was to put more staff into the passport office in answering Oireachtas queries. I just think that's mad, you know? That we have this system where people need to go to their TD to try and get [help], and then you have special staff in the passport office, answering us, about passports. It only arises because the state isn't doing what it's supposed to be doing.

These badly functioning systems get set up, which creates a role for keeping TDs important. It really shouldn't be necessary for the relatively small things like passports.

'Why do we need [people like] me to go to a special Oireachtas email line for whatever – for the HSE – why can't the public directly access it? These things are [gatekept] by TDs, not fully by choice, but by a series of choices made by the state. It shouldn't be necessary for someone to contact a TD to relate to the public service. That's really unique to Ireland.'

Though they were not his reason for entering politics – and Murphy says his focus remains on building community movements which try to exert pressure from outside, in tandem with his voice inside the Dáil – there remain some instances where constituency cases give him pride. One concerned a family, including a person with significant health challenges, whose landlord was about to sell their rental property. The local authority had considered buying the property to guarantee their continued tenure, then backed out because of the prospective management fees. Murphy was able to bring their case to the Residential Tenancies Board so that an immediate threat of eviction was staved off. Eventually, after he raised their case in the Dáil chamber itself as an example of insufficient laws on tenancy rights, the county council was convinced to offer the family a separate apartment, averting their material risk of homelessness. But can he even take credit for that? He's not sure: perhaps the council would have intervened either way. Maybe the publicity helped; maybe it was irrelevant.

If there were one thing he would change about Irish politics – and the author suspects he's not alone – it would be to remove this expectation that TDs are all-purpose fixers whom the public expect to mediate with public services. Much of a TD's constituency work, he says, is on matters that could be solved by browsing the website of the Citizens Information Board. Murphy's wife,

Jess Spear, was elected a councillor in 2024; Murphy finds a frustrating overlap in the work they're expected to do.

'I'm happy to help people, you know what I mean? But it is not a very efficient use of anyone's time – the idea that there's a section of the public services dealing with TDs, rather than actually just dealing with people, you know? That would make things work a lot better.'

If a TD's calling card is simply being good at navigating public services, he concludes, then there is no prevailing purpose to their life in politics. 'It would force politics to be more ideological, as well – you know, that you can't just win [a seat] on the basis that you're the best fella for getting a hip operation.'

ß

Many in Leinster House might baulk at the parochial or clientelist nature of the work members are expected to do, but for others it is an accepted part of the job.

Gary Gannon of the Social Democrats – representing the same Dublin Central constituency so effectively managed by Bertie Ahern's operation – gives an interview as he is awaiting a Dáil slot to raise concerns about the number 11 bus service, which is due to be replaced by two separate routes that require a change at Mountjoy Square. Gannon found this classic meat-and-potatoes constituency issue was emerging on the doors as canvassing stepped up for the 2024 election, when a usual twice-weekly canvass was stepping up to a nightly affair. Written parliamentary questions were tabled; residents' associations were informed and brought into the loop. He had put down a Topical Issue debate for the Dáil, the video of which would be shared afterwards.

'If we do live in a representative democracy, I do – where it's in keeping with my values – have to represent that particular viewpoint as I'm getting it. But don't get me wrong, there is also [the aspect of] letting people know that I'm doing it, and being people's advocate in the Dáil. Videos of mine go into local residents' groups, workshops, and all of that sort of stuff now, which is very modern. That's also letting people know that I'm doing it.'

5

THE RULES OF THE CLUB

'Garret used to hate them,' says one longtime inhabitant of Leinster House, referring to the former taoiseach Garret FitzGerald.
The two-term taoiseach of the 1980s would feel like he was having a good week, achieving wonderful things on behalf of his
country ... before going into the weekly meeting of Fine Gael
TDs and senators, and being promptly taken down a peg or two.

These weekly meetings of parliamentary parties (colloquial-
ly the 'PP') offer a path for a new, ambitious TD to make their
mark, and to try and impress upon others the need for solutions
to their chosen grievances. Whether in government or opposition, and whether parties are bigger operations with designated
spokespersons or smaller affairs where everyone pitches in, the PP
is a bread-and-butter option to communicate the need for action.

That, at least, is the premise. Those who have been there are
slightly less convinced about their ability to act as a truthful forum for honest back-and-forth about the direction of the party,
and in some cases the country.

'It has always been somewhat dysfunctional,' says one longtime deputy. 'They can be very good – some people have fan-
tastic antennae, and pick up things that might be going wrong
long before others, so they can be very effective in recognising the
problems that lie ahead.

'But you are only as good as whoever is speaking in the meeting: some people come in, a little bit like a lumpy old pillow,
bearing the imprint of the last person that lay upon it. You'll have

someone coming in giving some kind of Shakespearean soliloquy – this Joycean stream of consciousness – about the last thing they saw in a newspaper, or some off-the-wall thing a constituent has brought to them.'

It is for this reason that meetings do not simply become an open town hall forum, but have to be broken into a series of more organised, coherent pieces. 'People like to be able to sound off, and everyone gets their say, but others then complain that it's a stitch-up because you're not talking about the specific thing they want you to.'

Another TD speaks of their own disillusionment, arriving into the parliamentary party rooms expecting to have the ear of the great and the good – and realising the truth was a little more stage-managed and mundane. 'You expect to go into this magnificent forum, where epic political battles happen and people truly speak their minds. That doesn't happen. Instead it tends to be a way for people to just air their grievances into a silently nodding void. It's also the same handful of members speaking over and over again – because [other] members are often afraid of falling out with leadership or being seen as a pain, so they stay silent mostly, or make fairly anodyne remarks. Honest debate just doesn't happen, though people will say otherwise.'

From this perspective, party meetings often fall short on one major front: access to the front bench, and the ability to have input on big issues, is the *quid pro quo* for adopting the party whip in the first place.

♗

The 'whip' system is the bread and butter of how most parliamentary systems work. Commanding a majority of seats in a chamber like the Dáil only does so much: a government still cannot reliably pass laws unless it can be assured that all of its elected representatives will show enough discipline to vote precisely as the government wishes.

Such discipline is assured by organising the affairs of the Oireachtas so that individual politicians effectively need the party's supports to get any meaningful work done, and lose all those supports if members do not vote as the party leadership demands. The term 'whip' is inherited from Westminster, where it was borrowed from hunting parlance: a huntsman's assistant would surround a pack of hunting dogs and use the whip to stop any from straying from the pack.

Despite its role in creating the system, Westminster does not exercise that system quite as rigidly as the Dáil does. There, only the most pressing and important business is subject to a 'three-line whip' (the vote in question is, literally, underlined three times on a bulletin sent to MPs in advance), in which case defying the party's voting instructions will result in being expelled from the parliamentary grouping and being left to operate as a *de facto* independent MP. On other issues, a certain degree of defiance might be permissible: the party might turn a blind eye if an MP cannot reconcile their constituency's interests with the government's policy. At worst, this simply means MPs who routinely oppose the party's central stance will hamper their own prospects of promotion in future. A similar soft policy applies in the European Parliament and in the United States, where at worst an MEP or congressperson might hamper their prospects of a committee chairmanship.

Ireland, however, applies the whip with equal rigour almost all of the time. Every single deputy is expected to vote uniformly on every matter, whether it be something as significant as the appointment of a taoiseach or as relatively mundane as approving the agenda for the week's sitting.

'It's a necessary evil,' says one party whip (confusingly, the word 'whip' can mean both the voting instruction issued to members and the party TD responsible for enforcing this instruction). 'Partly because the margins can be fairly narrow – you could have a government with a majority of two or three, so if you let TDs have a free vote on something like a finance bill [legislation to give effect to tax changes announced in a budget] the whole thing would collapse very easily.'

But why, then, does the whip apply so rigidly in all instances? 'Where do you draw the line?' replies this whip. 'Do you let people vote however they like on legislation? You can't take the risk of letting people have a free vote on amendments to a complicated bill, in case there's some unexpected legal consequence.' Even the weekly vote to adopt a pre-published schedule of business for the week is too sensitive to be left to chance: the rules of the Dáil are so structured that if the Dáil has not pre-agreed its own agenda, it simply does not sit. A government that wants to get things done, therefore, must not only ensure TDs vote in favour of its bills – the voting discipline has to go further and ensure the schedule is exactly as the government wants it.

Only on the rarest instances is the whip lifted, and TDs offered a 'free vote' on an issue before the Dáil. This is usually only countenanced on what are generally billed as 'conscience issues' – matters like abortion or assisted suicide on which a party might not have a clearly defined position, thus leaving it up to members themselves to determine a future course of action.

Whips (the people) are also responsible for liaising with each other to arrange the week's business in the Dáil and Seanad – and for managing the attendance at each vote, communicating with members in advance to make sure all bodies are accounted for. This isn't always easily done for government ministers, whose work will often require overseas travel, most commonly to Brussels for summits with their EU counterparts. In these cases, whips have to make a case for an opponent on the opposition benches *not* to vote. This is known as 'pairing' – the minister who has good reason to be absent from the chamber will have their absence off-set by an opposition TD who skips the vote to maintain the usual everyday balance of government and opposition.

'We'd be goosed if we didn't have that system,' says the whip. 'It's a surprisingly honourable system. If we tell the leader of the opposition that the taoiseach has to be abroad, they'll abstain.' Otherwise, a government with a narrow majority could end up losing some Dáil votes, and in an extreme case even collapsing, simply because a minister was abroad on official business. In rare instances, opposition parties will make a principled point of with-drawing any pairing arrangements in protest at the government's handling of specific issues – with the awkward consequence of forcing ministers to abandon international engagements.

This also occurs whenever the Dáil is voting on a motion of confidence: the constitutional significance of the business means the entire ranks must be assembled. When a motion of no con-fidence was tabled in Helen McEntee in late 2023, following se-vere rioting and looting in central Dublin, environment minister Eamon Ryan was faced with the possibility of having to fly home from a UN climate summit in Dubai. Only when the penny dropped about the mortifying consequence – an environment minister making a round trip of over 7,000 miles simply to par-ticipate in one Dáil vote – was the protocol dispensed with. The Social Democrats agreed to offer a pair so that Ryan could remain in the UAE as a chief negotiator for the EU.

Nonetheless, sometimes TDs do have to make long-distance journeys simply to participate in Dáil business. In June 2024 two Fianna Fáil TDs, and a party senator, were invited to China ow-ing to their status on the Ireland–China Parliamentary Friendship Group. Some important Dáil business emerging, Micheál Martin summoned the Dáil duo of James O'Connor and Pádraig O'Sulli-van home for the votes. The pair had already engaged in freelance whipping and arranged their own pairs before travel but nonetheless diligently flew home to ensure the government was at its full strength for the votes. O'Connor, who convenes the Friendship Group, returned to China as soon as the votes were disposed of – a return journey of 10,000 miles.

Ω

If voting discipline is the proverbial stick, then the ability to be part of the inner circle is the carrot. For starters, being suspended from a parliamentary party denies someone the chance to attend the weekly PP meeting and the possibility of a minister paying attention to their grievances. A further exclusion comes in having their pre-assigned Dáil seat moved: TDs are assigned to seats for the purposes of electronic voting, but someone who has been kicked out of the parliamentary party will soon find their whip has transferred their vote to a vacant seat on the other side of the chamber. Even the idle moments ahead of a Dáil vote can no longer be used for networking, or to press a specific case with a minister.

But the influence of parliamentary parties goes a step further: the strength of parties determines the number of seats they can claim on individual Oireachtas committees, and the early months of a new Dáil involve a lot of horse-trading where whips try to assign party TDs to the committees that best reflect their interests, concerns and capabilities. (The Oireachtas Transport Committee, for example, often includes plenty of TDs from constituencies that house an airport.) Having made their case to be assigned to a committee that mirrors their own agenda, a TD suspended by their party might end up losing their spot on that committee. If that TD was the chair of that committee, they'll also lose out on the €10,000 annual allowance that went with the position.

There are other consequences too – the party's press office will no longer be available for the TD to publicise their affairs;

the backroom research and administrative staff can no longer be availed of if wanted.

There are two especially potent punishments, however. One is the loss of Dáil speaking time: when speaking slots are assigned and filled by the party whips, a deputy without a whip cannot get a slot. This means that, when the House is debating legislation, a TD outside the party fold simply cannot get speaking time. (The only mercy may be shown by the Ceann Comhairle, who, if there are sufficient numbers, might allow two minutes' grace for un-affiliated TDs to chip in at the tail end of a discussion.) In an industry where visibility matters, being gagged for proceedings on the Dáil floor is fatal.

The other issue concerns office assignments. Much like spaces on committees, members' offices are assigned by the party whips, who are assigned a block of offices commensurate with their num-bers of TDs and senators. A TD who leaves the fold can expect to find packing boxes left in their office quickly. Aontú founder Peadar Tóibín, suspended from Sinn Féin after opposing legisla-tion on abortion (the party had a pre-agreed position and could not offer a free vote), and who then quit the party entirely, stayed put in his office on the Sinn Féin corridor until a party official left packing boxes in his office one morning and instructed him to 'fuck off out of this area'. Former Labour senator James Hef-fernan, who lost the whip after voting against an element of the Social Welfare Bill in 2012, found the locks had literally been changed on the office he shared with a former party colleague.

'We're basically lobby fodder,' says one backbencher. 'We vote as we're told, and in exchange we get to use – or try to use – the internal machinery of the party. It's not much of a trade-off really.'

'It's a big sword that hangs over your head,' says another. 'The price you pay for being part of the club is that your loyalty is sup-posed to be to the club.'

When most politicians have exchanged their agency for access, the parliamentary party meetings should in principle be an important forum – and, in the past, were surrounded by a veil of silence. What happened in the party rooms stayed in the party rooms, and only matters of genuine national importance – like the election of a new party leader, as happened with Fianna Fáil in 1979 when Charles Haughey narrowly defeated George Colley to become leader and taoiseach – would ever seep out. Until the advent of the new millennium, this system largely worked well: there were only a handful of daily newspapers, RTÉ was the country's only licenced broadcaster, and the internet had not yet created a culture of needing all-day, 24-hour content to feed its growing user base. Save for the legendary Fianna Fáil heaves of the 1980s, there simply wasn't an appetite for the internal gossip of political parties. There were enough 'big picture' stories to keep the press busy.

'I remember,' a TD from a smaller party opines, 'when there'd be a leak from a Fianna Fáil PP – it would literally be front-page news. "Oh my God! There's a leak from a parliamentary party!" Now you might as well have them on telly.'

The evolution of media and the continual demands for new 'content' – plus the evolution of governments in the 2000s, with Fine Gael's decade bookended by leadership heaves and Fianna Fáil's empire undermined by economic tumult and threats to the viability of Brian Cowen's government – changed the dynamic entirely. By 2009 and 2010, with the government shovelling billions into the banking sector under the terms of the 2008 bank guarantee, it seemed like the fate of the country might hang on whether there was an active attempt to unseat Cowen as Fianna Fáil leader; more than once there were tales of Cowen giving 'the speech of his life' to reinforce the support of a fraying party. Also in 2010,

Fine Gael reckoned with the prospect that longtime leader Enda Kenny might squander the opportunity to win the subsequent election and instituted a heave. Kenny prevailed in a vote of parliamentary members, the result of which was known only to the two members who counted the votes. Over such internal divisions can the torch of power be passed.

There can be such paranoia about leaks from PP meetings that in the gravest of moments, where the future of leaders might be in the balance, there are instructions to leave phones outside of the room. One such occasion was in February 2017, when Enda Kenny was facing grave questions about his handling of Garda whistleblower complaints. Kenny having already announced he would be retiring at some point during that term, Fine Gael feared the collapse of the government and the onset of a general election under a lame-duck leader. TDs and senators arriving at the party rooms for the weekly meeting on Wednesday afternoon were instructed to leave their phones in a basket at the door, thus ensuring that there could be no real-time relay of information outside the room. Yet, despite the room being in virtual lockdown, RTÉ's David Davin-Power was able to inform the nation that Kenny had promised to deal with his future 'effectively and conclusively after Patrick's Day'; 'he got an ovation and the meeting moved on'. In the land of the blind, the one-eyed man is king: Kenny had a staff member in the room who could correspond with the outside world when his would-be critics were silenced. Pre-emptively disarming everyone else in the room meant there could be no undermining of his presentation.

The bubble of impenetrability was forever popped during the Covid-19 pandemic. Where previously it was taboo to spend the meeting glued to a phone – making it fairly obvious who a prospective leaker might be – the pandemic meant meetings could only take place online, via the likes of Zoom or Microsoft Teams. Suddenly, live commentary was the fare of the day; not alone would TDs, senators and MEPs be on the call, but so too might their office staff. Moreover, leaking was now exceptionally easy. 'You'd have Zoom in one window and WhatsApp in another,' says a staff member for a Fianna Fáil TD. Leaking became so routine, and the leaks so regular, that meetings might as well have been live-streamed. One political correspondent was so busy repeating the gossip being shared that they posted a tweet claiming, 'I spoke particularly strongly on that one' – pasting a source's WhatsApp message without changing the pronouns in their sentence.

For party members, this had both its upsides and its downsides. Comments that were previously made for internal consumption now had a wider audience: a vigorous or impassioned speech on any specific idea would now be remarked upon, in real time, by half a dozen colleagues and quickly relayed by the distant but curious media. Contributions suddenly became performative. 'People always speak differently when it's for internal consumption,' opines one who experienced both physical and virtual PP meetings. 'The tone definitely shifted when the meetings went online, and the public were effectively listening in, in real time. Suddenly it wasn't just enough to make a point – the leaks would also include people's opinions on whether you did or didn't make the point very well. It wasn't just what you said, but how you said it. People would end up playing to the gallery, except the gallery were only getting the news thirdhand!'

Playing to an external gallery cuts both ways. Richard Bruton concluded his parliamentary career as the chair of Fine Gael's parliamentary party. 'There's a bit of people feeling that they don't want to say what they would like to say, because they know it will be reported outside the room. So it is a bit self-defeating, that [performative] element of it.'

Bruton had been a TD for 42 years, witnessing both ends of the private/public era of parliamentary party meetings. His personal preference is for workshop-style gatherings, where members break off into smaller groups – which would have the purpose of disincentivising leaks, because the source would be so easily fingered – but found that other members didn't enjoy them as much, seeing the breakout groups as akin to silos ('We have them at the away day think-ins,' says one TD, 'and it feels pointless if your group doesn't include the minister for whichever issue it is').

'So you try different things,' says Bruton, 'but you do come back to this more theatrical forum, which I suppose mirrors the Dáil. And it does assure people that they get a chance to have the taoiseach hear the angst that they're experiencing, and so it fulfils that role very well – but it probably doesn't evolve into something greater.' Those who have deeper interests in specific areas, he found, tend to run solo and use backchannels to approach ministers instead of bringing it directly to the parliamentary party meeting.

Another downside to the *de facto* live broadcast of parliamentary party meetings is that off-colour comments which might otherwise have been brushed off are also disseminated as if they'd been said on live television. During one Fianna Fáil meeting during lockdown in January 2021, Marc MacSharry queried Ireland's stance against buying a Russian-engineered vaccine that was out of favour with the EU. 'If the Ku Klux Klan is selling a vaccine,' he told that meeting, 'we should buy it.' Some of those who heard the comment in real time understood it as a characteristically ebullient turn of phrase from one of Fianna Fáil's more colourful orators. Those who read it online didn't get the same impression. The blowback was so sudden and vigorous that MacSharry had already apologised, and withdrawn the comment, before the end of the meeting, saying there was 'no excuse for the use of such an analogy'.

When meetings returned in person, the dam could not be fully rebuilt: once a culture had been established of news coming out inevitably anyway, it was impossible to reestablish one of absolute secrecy. Now, while enterprising reporters will still try to find their own information, Fianna Fáil and Fine Gael circulate an end-of-meeting summary – effectively an auxiliary press release – outlining any motions that were passed, and any contributions made by the party leader. This is, objectively, a controlled and house-approved narrative of events intended to satiate the appetite for an immediate readout of what occurs behind closed doors. As the only 'official' record of events, it can also have a strategic purpose: the comments attributed to the party leader can be designed for mainstream dissemination, like staking a claim to priorities in a forthcoming budget, or signalling to coalition partners that certain ideas won't (or will) be acceptable. Coalescing parties can negotiate via semi-official briefings before ever having to sit down and determine their common future.

⚷

A point often remarked upon by figures inside Leinster House, and sometimes by those outside it, is the comparatively impregnable nature of meetings of the Sinn Féin parliamentary party. Political correspondents can always operate on the presumption that the other 'big two' parties will meet on a Wednesday, with gossip beginning to emanate afterwards. By comparison, the meetings of Sinn Féin may as well take place in the Sistine Chapel, for all the news that emerges from them.

Opponents in other parties like to portray this as a nefarious function of Sinn Féin's internal structures – alluding to some Belfast-headquartered backroom quietly pulling the strings and giving instructions to the Dublin-based party about what may or may not be acceptable conduct to the living combatants of the Troubles. This is an understandable take: a public inquiry into Northern Ireland's 'cash for ash' scandal heard evidence that Máirtín Ó Muilleoir, Sinn Féin's finance minister in the Stormont

Executive, asked for the approval of Ted Howell – a long-standing ally and confidant of Gerry Adams – before signing off on the business case for a cost-cutting proposal in 2017. Ó Muilleoir claimed the email was merely a courtesy to a lifelong Sinn Féin negotiator; others suggested it was to check that no arrangement would accidentally breach party policy. Opponents perceived party headquarters as still running the rule over elected office-holders in positions of authority; even literal members of a government were, they argued, still subject to the diktat of head office.

Sinn Féin members, on and off the record, dispute this perception – and have a much more benign reason for their meetings never producing news: they are simply newsless. 'They're pretty much just for housekeeping,' insisted one frontbencher. 'It's basically an all-staff meeting where we're all told what's coming up on the Dáil schedule, in private members' business or whatever. It's a chance for the whip to say, "Listen, lads, there was trouble getting people in for votes the last time; if I say there's votable business from four o'clock, I don't want you ringing me at four to say you're in trouble because you're stuck across town."' So procedural and mundane are these meetings, that member claimed, that they're also attended by parliamentary assistants and the party's central staff.

But if that's the case, what forum do party colleagues have to raise any grievances with each other – to pass on the anger from their constituents, to advise a frontbencher that their stance or commentary is going down poorly, to suggest alternatives, and to generally push the party into a more workable and popular direction? 'This is going to sound like *Little House on the Prairie* … it's not that we all love each other, but we do just all get along. If you feel like something is pissing off people in your area, you just go straight to them and say it. We're just a bit more relaxed about it.'

That culture may stem from the earlier eras when there were simply fewer Sinn Féin TDs in the building anyway. The first Sinn

Féin TD of the modern era was elected in 1997, and the party's Dáil representation only reached double figures in 2011. Smaller teams simply did not need formal gatherings to tell each other how they felt; this largely remains the case for Leinster House's smaller political outfits. Aside from occasional briefings to go over the coming days' business, and discussions on how a party will use its forthcoming allocation of private members' time, there is little need to set a standing appointment for members to get together.

For 'full-time' independent TDs, elected outside of organised parties, there is obviously no parliamentary party. Yet, because of the aforementioned protocols where speaking slots and committee positions are handed out to groupings, independent TDs – and those of smaller parties – have to form everyday groupings anyway.

These are known as 'technical groups', where a minimum number of five TDs come together to be treated ostensibly as if they were a party in the doling out of parliamentary speaking time and committee positions. In more recent years, there have been three such groups, formed loosely along ideological lines – one entailing rural conservatives, one with leftists from small parties and none, and a third involving provincial centrist and centre-right deputies. This practice means independents mostly end up self-affiliating with others of a similar mind; the Rural Independent Group of 2020–24 ended up spawning a formal political party, Independent Ireland, which got four deputies elected in the 2024 election. Eight centrist and centre-right independents clubbed together to form a negotiating bloc in early 2025 and ended up being included as a formal partner in a Fianna Fáil–Fine Gael coalition.

Being of similar mind is a practical prerequisite: when groups are allotted speaking time at Leaders' Questions, or offered their rostered time slot in which they can table their own business, it is helpful to have a similar outlook so that it's easier to reach consensus on how the slots should be used. Nonetheless, the groups often remain businesslike in tone, and will operate an internal rota system leaving a designated speaker free to raise whatever they like.

Such groups often provide for unlikely bedfellows. At the time of writing, the independent (and one-time Green) TD Paul Gogarty was briefly a member of the same technical group as Danny Healy-Rae, a climate-change denier who has decreed that 'God above is in charge of the weather'. These arrangements are purely transactional, however, for the mutual administrative benefit of being able to get a spot on the roster for Leaders' Questions and positions on committees. The more members a group can accrue, the greater its share of committee roles – and possibly of committee chairmanships too.

The involvement of committee positions does, however, mean some independents having to compromise on their independence. Even if voting discipline isn't expected, groups still have to nominate a whip to act as a convenor and a go-between with Oireachtas authorities – and to act as a liaison with other whips at meetings of the Business Committee. These whips are the gatekeepers to committee positions, so independent TDs must make their cases to their whips to get assigned to the committees that most interest them. Independent TDs therefore become co-dependent, and indeed interdependent, to maximise their own leverage. (When this irony is presented to one independent politician, the retort is clear: 'Better to find ways to work together than not to work at all.')

As with any workplace, however, technical groups produce their fair share of office politics – particularly in the presence of abrasive personalities that rub colleagues up the wrong way. Tipperary's Mattie McGrath, who convened the Rural Independent Group in 2020, irked his colleagues by routinely describing himself as its 'leader' in press releases – and at one point even recruited a 'general secretary' for the group, much to the bafflement of his colleagues who could discern neither any workload nor any logic for such a job. McGrath's first-among-equals approach so irked his colleagues that although every member of the group won re-election in 2024, they dispersed among other technical groups and, for some time, vetoed McGrath himself having any role within them. The Tipperary TD might have been one of the Dáil's most colourful speakers, but even his own colleagues felt they had heard a bit too much.

6

PASSING THE TIME

The key to retaining a seat in Leinster House, some rural TDs insist, is to be in Leinster House as little as possible.

Internal gossip groups keep tabs on all the out-of-towners who are spotted in Leinster House on a Friday, when the Dáil and Seanad aren't in session. Those who are spotted around the parliamentary complex on non-sitting days are broadly labelled as being uncommitted to their constituencies. The gossip eventually makes it back to party leadership, whose views on various figures might be coloured by the perception that a politician is getting too fond of the Leinster House lifestyle and not putting in the hard yards at home.

Such is the impossible job of being a public representative: most politicians want to spend time in their constituencies, but equally know that doing the *job* of a TD inevitably means having to be in Dublin, looking for meetings, firing off correspondence, contributing in the Dáil or sitting down in an Oireachtas committee room. Many of the tasks of the job are done in darkness, the menial tasks of quiet bureaucracy. Yet the public simultaneously wants their representative to be seen in the chamber, giving out yards about the state of the area, *and* for them to be seen out and about in the constituency itself.

But since Padre Pio has never been a member of Dáil Éireann – and debate may rumble on as to whether he would be able to command a quota in Foggia anyway – bilocation isn't an option, so something has to give. The resultant fudge is a three-day parliamentary week: Leinster House is busy from Tuesdays to Thursdays, but largely empty on Mondays and Fridays.

The distance of some members from Dublin has its knock-on consequences on how the Dáil does its business. Commuting to the city from some of the most westerly coastal areas is a slog, sometimes taking up to 5 hours: the commute of one-time Fine Gael TD Noel Harrington, from Castletownbere on Ireland's south-westerly tip, included so many winding rural roads that his return drive from Leinster House would only be half finished by the time he crossed the border back into Cork. While TDs living in Leinster would aspire to sleep in their own beds most nights – electing to choose home comforts and an early alarm over the rest of a sterile hotel bed – most in Munster, Connacht or Ulster simply don't see it as tenable to commute every day.

In the late 1980s, as the pay of a TD dramatically caught up with and then overtook that of the average worker – and as the capital became increasingly populated with apartments – many TDs from further afield bought themselves second homes in Dublin to transplant some domestic comforts during a long working week. More recent recruits are less comfortable with committing to a property purchase, and – despite their high salaries – have neither the income nor job stability to consider it anyway, and so city-centre hotels become their sanctuaries.

Politicians smile wryly when hearing concerns from tourists, foreign and domestic, about the rising cost of Dublin hotels – even on a weeknight, they themselves are equally pinched by the cost of a bed in the capital. Some have even abandoned the pursuit of a bed in Dublin and accept an even longer commute instead – a trend highlighted by ex-Fianna Fáil senator Eugene Murphy, who has admitted to sleeping in his car. Unwilling to meet the premium cost of a hotel anywhere in central Dublin, the senator intended to simply drive home to Roscommon after a late sitting, but felt so exhausted on the drive that he ended up pulling over in Mullingar and spending the night sleeping fitfully in his parked car at a petrol station forecourt.

ჸ

While naturally compromised by the desire of TDs to spend time in their constituencies, the scheduling of Dáil business is largely influenced by two factors: the desire to squeeze a full week of work into a three-day window, and the need to justify TDs' absence from home. The result is late finishes on Tuesday and Wednesday: it is not uncommon for the Dáil to sit until close to midnight on a Tuesday night, early until late on Wednesday, and again on Thursday from 9 a.m. until early in the evening. The timetable leaves space for the cabinet to hold its weekly meeting on a Tuesday morning, without ministers being sidetracked by Oireachtas business, and for members to get home on a Thursday afternoon or evening. Mondays and Fridays are therefore ring-fenced for the more routine clinics, meetings and visits of a constituency politician.

The notional starting and finishing times, however, don't tell the full story. The choreography and public face of the Dáil would lead you to think TDs are working at full blast for three long days – and, of course, if there is work to be done after the civil service has clocked off, they'll do it – but the evenings are often more idle than many will admit.

That's because the public perception of the Dáil is that it conducts 'debates', where a TD stands up and makes a point, which is then rebutted by someone on the other side, only for a third member to then make a counter-rebuttal or introduce a new supporting argument, and so on. A person who has never watched a parliamentary debate – and that's most people on planet Earth – might imagine the proceedings to resemble a school or college debating society. Indeed, many of those in Ireland's prominent college debating societies, like the Hist or the Phil in Trinity or the L&H or LawSoc in UCD, can imagine themselves making similarly impassioned and forceful interventions to move the needle in public life.

In short, that's rarely how it actually works. Leinster House debates are in reality more akin to a series of statements read in a vacuum, in which one TD stands up, reads from a script and sits down; another TD stands up, reads from a script and sits down; a third TD stands up and reiterates the same points, then sits down, and so on. (One significant reason why shouting matches get such disproportionate media attention and coverage is that they are the exception to the norm: mundane recitations of pre-written scripts are rarely stimulating and often barely newsworthy.)

One byproduct of this is that speaking time is also pre-allocated to certain members, and so TDs will know a few days in advance if they're likely to have an opportunity to contribute in the chamber. In an average 2-hour debate, about 20 TDs might have a chance to say a few words. So what do the rest do? Some will sit around for the debate, being personally invested in the topic at hand. Others will show up in the chamber to offer some semblance of moral support, which might conveniently result in them being seen on TV looking animated and supportive as their colleague makes their speech. For others, though, there isn't much to do. Dubliners without speaking slots might entertain the idea of nipping back to their constituencies, deal with some correspondence, or occupy themselves at a committee meeting.

Wednesday nights at least have a little more structure and a little more business. An overhaul of Dáil routines in 2016 resulted in Leinster House borrowing a model from the European Parliament and introducing a pre-scheduled 'voting block'. Where previously a vote might be triggered in the Dáil at any time – leaving TDs somewhat shackled, barely able to leave the environs of Leinster House for fear of being the crucial missing vote in an important division (a vote in the Dáil chamber) – the majority of votes are now deferred to a specific window. Originally this was scheduled for Thursday lunchtimes, but shifted to Wednesday evenings during the Covid-19 pandemic. As a result, other than on a Tuesday afternoon when TDs are asked to ratify the schedule of business for the rest of the week, almost every vote is now deferred until the same period on Wednesdays.

This idea was part of a conscious effort to make politicians' working hours slightly more compatible with family life, giving TDs certainty on when their votes might be sought, and liberating them from the paranoia of potentially being needed at the drop of a hat. Dubliners now have the possibility of leaving the complex to head home for a few hours, perhaps getting the kids fed and ready for bed, and returning on schedule to vote later that evening. That possibility, however, rarely if ever materialises: one Dublin-based TD said the window is so small, the traffic so heavy, and the schedule so fluid (with voting windows brought forward if previous business concludes early) that there is still no scope to leave.

On that front, there is an unspoken tension between TDs from inside and outside the Pale. The original Thursday voting session meant complications for rural deputies who liked, when possible, to get out of Dublin early on a Thursday morning and spend more valuable time in their constituencies. The complications of Covid-19, when the Dáil had to hold socially distanced sittings in the Convention Centre Dublin, resulted in votes being taken on Wednesday nights instead, an arrangement that has persisted ever since. Moving the voting time accidentally formalised the ability of rural TDs to get out of town early on Thursdays: if a long-driving member doesn't have a speaking slot in the chamber, or doesn't have a committee meeting to attend, it is now commonplace for them to 'fob in' on a Thursday to register their attendance for the purposes of qualifying for their full allowance, and then leave

Dublin altogether. (Some more conspiratorially minded denizens of Leinster House think there are extra shenanigans afoot here: office space in the Oireachtas complex is so constrained that independent TDs are often assigned to offices in the Department of Agriculture, which can facilitate 24-hour access, unlike Leinster House 'proper', which is locked up at night. There is a belief that some independents can therefore 'fob in' at a minute past midnight on Thursday morning, be recognised on the system as having attended the Oireachtas that day, and make their way home under cover of darkness.)

This restructuring of the Dáil schedule has a knock-on consequence on the rest of business: Thursday sittings are now skewed towards question-and-answer sessions and statements, with little or no legislation debated (a 'zombie session', as one whip says witheringly) when there are fewer members on the premises. Moreover, the work of the Dáil's various committees (34 at the time of writing, most with aspirations to meet weekly) is now compressed into a shorter working week, with the majority squeezed into Wednesday, and compressed into shorter sittings because of the increased demand on the four committee rooms.

From the perspective of time management, this might be seen as a more efficient way of getting work done, squeezing almost a full week's work into a hectic day and a half. But some believe lower quantity of time in Leinster House significantly undermines the quality of work that TDs are put there to do.

'If you're an opposition party or a government backbencher, and you're complaining with the lack of time being given to [considering] Report Stage amendments and all the rest, you can't then be in favour of vote blocking,' says one party whip. 'If people realised the amount of serious business, and how it's condensed, and how we don't get to [debate some] amendments, and how we don't actually tease out legislation, or debate it as thoroughly as we should – all because you want to go home on a Thursday morning? There should be anger about it – at the end of the day, as difficult and tough as this job is, it's a very privileged and important job.'

Scheduling a voting block is of little or no help to TDs from outside the Pale, who conversely find themselves resigned to hanging around on a Wednesday evening, possibly dawdling for a few hours waiting for some predetermined votes to work themselves through.

In any event, there is also an unspoken shame about the cramming of so many votes into a single window: TDs often simply don't know for certain, until a few moments in advance, what it is they're voting on. The job of the whips is to organise the business and to corral their deputies into backing the party's stance – but the business of a full week is so varied, leading to votes on a panoply of topics, and the votes so frequent within the block, that many in the chamber are simply flying blind. Is the vote at hand on a government motion, an opposition bill hoping to become law, or an amendment to a non-binding 'private members' motion' tabled by an opposition grouping? If it's the latter, who's proposing it, and where do other opposition parties stand on that? Do they support an alternative wording proposed from elsewhere on the floor?

The vast majority of Dáil votes take place electronically, with a 60-second window for TDs to press the green (*Tá*) or red (*Níl*) buttons on a panel beside their seat, or a blue (*Staon*) button if they want to register a formal abstention. This option is relatively novel in Dáil votes, introduced only in 2016, in recognition of Fianna Fáil's arrangement to abstain on key votes so that Fine Gael's minority government could prevail. In the absence of an official button, there was no formal way for TDs to register their ambivalence on a matter – they were simply recorded as not participating in the vote, and might as well have been absent entirely.

Such is the flurry of votes, however, that many TDs will bide their time in the first few seconds, and watch the two big screens mounted on the chamber walls, which act as makeshift scoreboards. Only when the bulbs corresponding to the front row seat are illuminated, signalling the position of the various party leaders and whips, will many backbenchers follow their lead.

ƹ

Padre Pio might have a role, though, in another more recent proposal to make the Dáil's working schedule more family friendly – not just for politicians, but for the support staff who have to work to the politicians' schedules. One novel idea is to effectively have the Dáil sit in two places at once: the last Ceann Comhairle, Seán Ó Fearghaíl, conceived an arrangement where the 'main' chamber could continue its business debating proposed new laws, while a parallel smaller chamber ('the Dáil-in-committee') could dispose of other matters like ministerial question time, or Topical Issues discussions, where votes are not involved and the attendance of the entire house is therefore not needed. The simple hypothesis was that if the Dáil were to sit twice at the same time, TDs might be able to finish up and go home earlier.

But many politicians simply don't think that would work: if many TDs still lived too far away to commute, and were therefore going to stay in Dublin for two midweek nights anyway, wouldn't they end up organising more business to keep themselves occupied? Politicians with younger families on the cusp of commuting distance would find it difficult to convince their families that their presence was needed up in Dublin – and might perversely end up arranging extra parliamentary business to justify their absence from home. The end result would be that instead of having one chamber sitting late two evenings a week, there would be two. What's more, ministers whose schedules are already a masterclass in logistical organisation might find themselves coming under even greater pressure to stay in Leinster House and entertain the concerns of backbenchers raising some local issue with the national platform.

Without any great chorus or fanfare, therefore, the idea was quietly shelved. Leinster House's reading room, earmarked as the auxiliary second chamber, was allowed to remain, albeit with a much more stripped-down aesthetic. TDs might have wanted to organise their business a little better, but as with many other aspects of life in Leinster House, the broken system remains for want of a consensus on how to fix it.

7

DOWN THE CORRIDOR

Find a random person on the street and show them a photograph of Leinster House, or ask a taxi driver about the building at the Kildare Street end of Molesworth Street, and they will tell you that the building is 'Dáil Éireann'. Protests will often bill themselves as taking place outside the Dáil; press officers will sometimes arrange photocalls with non-TDs outside 'the gates of the Dáil'.

This is not incorrect but it's only partly true. Of course, Leinster House is the home of the Dáil, where the TDs directly elected by the public gather to transact the business of the country. But Leinster House is officially the home of the Houses of the Oireachtas, including not just the Dáil, but the forgotten wing of Irish lawmaking: the Seanad.

The very need for a second parliamentary chamber itself has long been debated, and its existence is partly the result of institutional inertia and partly the fingerprint of Britain's involvement in setting up the institutions of the modern Irish state.

When the Irish Republic was first declared in 1919, the secessionist Sinn Féin MPs meeting in Dublin to form their own all-island parliament saw no need for a second chamber. This new republic was simply ignored by Britain, which in 1920 tried to re-enforce its own governance on the island – while defusing the tensions between the secessionist Catholic majority and the more loyal Protestant minority – by splitting Ireland in two. The six north-eastern counties, with the largest Protestant and Unionist populations, would become Northern Ireland; the remainder would become 'Southern Ireland'. As a project in managing tensions it was about as fruitful as giving two bickering children their own separate bedrooms: it might stop them fighting at nighttime, but does little to stop the more rebellious child from wanting to run away entirely.

Each part of partitioned Ireland was to have a legislature that, being designed by the British, closely resembled Westminster itself, with a house of commons and a senate mirroring the role of the House of Lords. In the case of Southern Ireland, this senate was to include four Catholic bishops, two Protestant bishops, 14 provincial representatives of county councils, 16 lords or members of the landed gentry, and 17 'Representatives of Commerce (including Banking), Labour, and the Scientific and Learned Professions)'.

Southern Ireland was a doomed experiment, and existed only on paper for a few months before Britain agreed to negotiate an Irish Free State, the precursor to today's republic, with an arm's-length relationship to London. This *de facto* merger between Southern Ireland and the Irish Republic, under British stewardship, meant the Free State would again replicate the structures of Britain: new proposals would need the approval of the Dáil and the senate, and get the assent of the king, before becoming law. The senate, now taking the title of Seanad Éireann, was to be made up of citizens who had 'done honour to the Nation by reason of useful public service or that, because of special qualifications or attainments, they represent important aspects of the Nation's life'.

All of which is to say that the Seanad was conceived as a sort of 'council of elders', in a similar vein to the House of Lords in London – but because it fell to TDs to fill half of the first seats, what was conceived as a genteel thinktank quickly became a partisan battlefield, with many seats being given to party allies. The other half of the seats were filled by the government of the day, which appointed a large number of southern unionists and Anglo-Irish aristocrats in a nod to the new state's mixed political heritage. This ended up being its Achilles' heel: by the time Eamon de Valera's Fianna Fáil got to power in 1932, 10 years after the Seanad was first composed, there was a huge culture clash between the two chambers. The Statute of Westminster had weakened London's grip over the rest of the empire, and de Valera had won an election on a platform of republicanising the Free State, abolishing royal insignia and oaths of allegiance. The unionists in the Seanad were concerned about antagonising London, and tried to frustrate the plans by delaying their implementation (the Seanad had no veto) as much as possible. Unmoved, in 1934 de Valera simply tried to abolish the Seanad entirely, and overcame the resistance of senators themselves to see the chamber disbanded in 1936.

A new Seanad Éireann was created in a new constitution a year later – which itself was also the fruit of de Valera's attempts to take Britain's fingerprints off the state – but with the key difference that the taoiseach of the day would now personally appoint 11 of the 60 members, all but guaranteeing that the prevailing government could push through whatever business it liked. Six of the remaining 49 seats would be elected by the graduates of the two universities, and 43 by 'vocational' panels similar to those imagined for Southern Ireland: culture and education; agriculture and fisheries; labour, industry and commerce; and public administration. The electorate for these vocational panels would be the existing members of the Oireachtas and the members of city and county councils – thus again ensuring that the 'council of elders' model would come secondary to party political expediency, with candidates being elected primarily for the colour of their rosettes and not their competence as scrutineers of legislation.

In a lofty sense, the Seanad has sought to cherish the legacy of the 1920s by billing itself as a forum where minority voices have a better chance of representation, free from the majoritarian tyranny of the universal franchise. Its 2022 centenary programme carried the slogan 'minority voices, major changes', highlighting the likes of David Norris, who might never have been able to get elected to the Dáil on the same gay rights platform that he was able to articulate in the upper house. The manner in which Seanad seats are filled leaves space for figures outside the jurisdiction: seats are now often taken by party members from Northern Ireland, and recent senators have included Armagh unionist farmer Ian Marshall, and Chicago restaurateur Billy Lawless as a nod to the diaspora. Meanwhile, Edith Costello, W.B. Yeats and Douglas Hyde, as members of the very first senate in the 1920s, argued in favour of the new Free State recognising divorce – an unthinkable concept given the social supremacy of Catholic doctrine at the time. At the time of writing, members include Eileen Flynn, the first Irish Traveller to serve in the Oireachtas, nominated by then-taoiseach Micheál Martin in 2020 as a non-party figure agreeable to all coalition parties.

The institutional capture of the Seanad by political parties leaves the chamber in a curious position: while on paper it has the standing of a full house of parliament, a huge number of its members would rather not be there. Senatorial elections are held three months after elections to the Dáil, leaving the Seanad as a fall-back option for defeated candidates who want a second crack at life in Leinster House. Party headquarters will play a role, identifying near-miss Dáil candidates who might stand a chance of getting elected in the future, and encouraging councillors to prioritise them on the ballot paper. Their prospects are challenged by the presence of outgoing TDs who have just lost their seats, whose careers are on the wane, leaving them facing immediate unemployment, and who will take a Seanad seat as the next best option – even if it means squeezing out some younger colleague whose career might be blossoming. The upper house is simultaneously a political crèche and a parliamentary retirement home.

Only a handful of senators are actually content to make the Seanad a long-term home. The six senators elected from university panels generally run because their interests are truly national and not specific to a geographical constituency. The majority of the others are in something of a holding pattern, waiting for the next opportunity to get back into the bigger chamber at the southern end of Leinster House. This also means the Seanad can have a relatively high turnover of members: many will only be happy to serve one term in the chamber, as for most candidates in major parties, two successive defeats in a general election will usually mark the end of their national career.

𐂸

Those who aspired to arrive in the Dáil, and who end up in the Duke of Leinster's former ballroom at the other end of the corridor, can be consoled by the Seanad's lesser workload. The constitution stipulates that the government is accountable to the Dáil, and makes no similar comment about the Seanad. The upper house therefore does not have the same routine access to ministers, nor daily Q&A sessions with the taoiseach. Its primary task is to scrutinise proposed legislation working its way through the parliamentary system. This in turn means that if the government simply isn't producing new bills for scrutiny, or if a backlog has built up in the Dáil with nothing for senators to get to work on, the sitting week can be a relatively short one. The House will convene on a Tuesday lunchtime and sit until mid-evening, do a full day's work on Wednesday, and often adjourn again by Thursday lunchtime. Sometimes, if the calendar requires the chamber to be used for other purposes like a committee meeting, the working week can end on Wednesday afternoon, little more than 24 hours after it began.

Senators therefore have much more scope to entertain additional careers outside of politics, or indeed to be more active presences in their own constituencies should the Seanad be a temporary stop on their professional journey to the Dáil. Despite the light workload, the job still carries an attractive salary of over €76,000, plus travel and accommodation allowances. Altogether, not a bad deal for members who can confidently plan to do other things on Mondays, Fridays, Tuesday mornings and most Thursday afternoons.

In the interests of balance, it should be noted that the Seanad's lighter workload is not entirely of its own choosing. The proposed abolition of the Seanad, narrowly rejected by voters in a referendum in 2014, seemed to push it to re-examine its role in public life and find a specific niche that would differentiate it from the better-known Dáil. Some have proposed that senators should replicate their American cousins and adopt a role in scrutinising, or even blocking, the appointment of judges or the chairs of state agencies. Others have tried to engineer set-piece occasions with outside guest speakers: the Dáil might never hear an address from the Lord Mayor of Belfast, or the President of the GAA, but the Seanad will happily find the time to do so.

Some senators, who estimate that around two-thirds of new Irish law is ultimately derived from Brussels, are keen to see the Seanad specialising in scrutiny of European law. Ireland has been lax in using powers under the EU's Lisbon Treaty, adopted in 2009, which allow national parliaments to show a 'yellow card' to any European initiative that risks trespassing on national powers. Yet a concrete plan to fill this void was also frustrated: a committee set up in 2023 with the goal of scrutinising Ireland's adoption of EU directives was simply told that the government officials who draft the wording of legislation were not willing to share their drafts.

'The senate could be so useful in affirming public appointments,' says one longtime member, 'or on EU scrutiny, on that six-week opportunity to send back a view … but it is the executive of the day, the government of the day, who opt to keep the senate toothless.'

Despite efforts to find its niche, and to make itself useful in Irish life, the Seanad has found itself as a solution in search of a problem.

R

There are a few illustrations of the Seanad's role as the lesser of the two Houses in Leinster House. The first is salary: while the base pay of a TD has now risen into six figures, senators usually earn just under three-quarters of the same amount, and are also paid a lower travel allowance. This is to reflect the official position that a senator is not representative of any specific geographical constituency, much as many may pretend otherwise. It is routine for senators, if they intend to run in the next general election, to describe themselves as the 'senator for county X' and look to place themselves on the same electoral plane as a TD. However, because senators do not enjoy a mandate from those same constituencies, they are not given the same public funding to support their travel around their home turf as a deputy is given.

Another discrepancy is in the staffing assignment. Whereas TD are given two full-time staff from the public purse, senators get a sole administrative assistant, whose pay is only around half of their own. Having only one member of support staff can leave senators feeling particularly exposed, and it has been known for some members to pool their staff so that, for example, two senators each cover half the wage of two assistants who can then stagger their annual leave. One former assistant believes many senators are haunted by an inferiority complex, given their lesser standing relative to TDs, and some simply like the notion of having 'staff', plural, to soothe their egos.

Perhaps the biggest illustration of the Seanad's lesser standing is the level of media attention paid to its affairs. For many years the only coverage of the upper house was by Jimmy Walsh of the *Irish Times*, who would commonly file far more copy on the chamber's proceedings than the newspaper would publish. His retirement in 2013 meant there were no dedicated reporters covering the beat of the House. Television coverage is equally scant, and the office televisions in the various media workspaces are only ever tuned to the Seanad floor if reporters have been given reason to expect a sparky remark.

While a newsworthy exchange in the Dáil will be quickly picked up on and shared, it often falls to senators themselves to publicise the more remarkable comments from the floor. A particularly salty, sarky or cutting exchange will probably be shared on the member's X or Instagram account, and spotted by the media shortly afterwards. Otherwise, the thick-carpeted floors of the Seanad chamber almost work as inadvertent soundproofing for a chamber which is often left to serve itself. If the old Westminster quip is true that the best way to keep a secret is by announcing it in the House of Lords, that chamber's Irish equivalent might well be similarly efficient at keeping information to a small audience.

ʔ

The varied ways in which the Seanad is filled means different members are playing to different galleries. The six university senators can be elected with thousands, if not tens of thousands, of votes, and will often dedicate themselves to politics of a solely national nature. Many doubt there would be a geographical constituency for the likes of Rónán Mullen, the longtime senator elected by graduates of the National University of Ireland, a former communications official for the Archdiocese of Dublin who is unapologetic in reflecting conservative traditions and in opposing anything overtly progressive or 'woke'. Likewise, the likes of David Norris or Lynn Ruane, two mainstays returned by the University of Dublin (i.e. Trinity College, which is the only component of that university), might never have been elected to the Dáil representing national liberal platforms that had no explicit concern for the constituencies in which they would run. A senatorial life, with no geographical links and no specific need to tend to local matters, is almost tailor made for such contributions.

The majority of senators – 43 across 5 vocational panels – have an electorate of about 1,100, the majority of whom are members of local authorities. While the Dáil is packed with people trying to say or do the popular thing in the pursuit of retaining their seats, those in the Seanad will often find themselves obsessing over matters in which the public is not at all invested. Prime among these are the pay and conditions of local authority members: barely a month goes by without a senator speaking up about the relatively low pay of councillors, or the fact that their paltry wage is subject to a class of PRSI contributions for which they receive literally nothing. One councillor-turned-TD had a routine dental visit after their election, and was aghast to learn that the free exam available to almost every other worker in the country was not covered by their own unique class of social insurance.

Those motivations also explain some of the rare instances in which the Seanad pushes back on government plans. The rules of the Dáil do not lend themselves to TDs mounting a filibuster, but in the Seanad the idea of strategically talking down the clock so as to artificially elongate and stifle debate is a little more of a fine art. At the time of writing, the most recent filibuster – mounted by government members against their own cabinet's legislation – was on a policing bill that included a plan to abolish joint policing committees, forums through which councillors can have a material input in how gardaí operate in their areas.

The bill's passage in the Dáil was routine and unremarkable, but Fianna Fáil senators became particularly vexed at this diminution of democracy and intervened one after another with slightly spurious procedural questions, eventually delaying business for so long that a final vote could not take place before the scheduled end to that day's business. Members freely admitted afterwards that their council colleagues (who are also their voters) were unhappy about losing their influence over local policing, and while coalition practicalities meant they couldn't stand up and openly criticise a minister from their own government, strategic suppression of the debate was the next best thing. The stalling tactic was, at least, enough to bring about further backroom consultation with the government about the impact on councillors' roles, and for some favour to be banked for the future. Even with the byzantine electoral structures of the Seanad, all politics is local.

That filibuster, mercifully, only went on for one evening. Some senators have been known to be so indulgent in their inputs – and so opposed to the whims of a government – that some legislation has simply withered and died before getting the chance to pass into law. The best example is a bill overhauling the structure for appointing judges, published in 2017, but which took over a year to get through the Dáil before its arrival in the Seanad. There, it met with sustained opposition from a handful of senators (led by the former attorney general Michael McDowell) who simply thought the legislation had become too complex, internally contradictory and ultimately entirely impracticable. That was a point they were happy to make, repeatedly, across 40 different sittings in 12 months, stringing out debate on the legislation across a full calendar year. Accounting for all stages of debate, the Seanad managed to squeeze 18 months out of a single bill. Critics wearily pointed out that tying up the minister for justice in the Seanad chamber for such a long time kept him away from working on plenty of other more popular ideas.

The final 11 members are the taoiseach's nominees, who effectively have a constituency of 1. They are appointed by whoever becomes taoiseach after the corresponding Dáil is elected, though the 11 positions are ordinarily divided among the parties in coalition in proportion to their sizes in the Dáil. Constitutionally these exist so that the government of the day will almost certainly have an inbuilt majority: the architects of the constitution wanted to avert the (admittedly unlikely) prospect of a Washington-style deadlock where the two Houses of the Oireachtas might be controlled by rival parties or groupings.

These positions are often a second, and sometimes a third, bite of the cherry for the nominees: the jobs are generally given to those who have shown promise in the previous general election, and who might have further successful tilts ahead of them. A candidate who withdrew from the general election so as to avoid a constituency split, or one who was added by party headquarters to act as a 'sweeper' collecting votes from one area on the premise of transferring them to another, might be rewarded for their duties. Others who polled well, and who were unfortunate not to gain Dáil seats, will be appointed to learn the ropes and maintain a national profile.

The staggered timing of elections – with senatorial elections taking place three months after Dáil ones – sometimes means these jobs can be handed out more freely. Should a taoiseach's nominee be elected to the Dáil, their Seanad position falls vacant and can be filled by the incumbent taoiseach at the stroke of a pen for the few weeks in which that outgoing Seanad remains in situ. These 'weekend senator' positions – so called because the recipients have barely arrived in the job before losing it again – are among the most exclusive baubles that any taoiseach can gift.

Fianna Fáil's victory in 2007 saw four of the previous taoiseach's nominees winning seats in the Dáil, leaving four vacancies for Bertie Ahern to hand out as post-electoral rewards. One of the seats was given to Seán Dorgan, Fianna Fáil's new general secretary, who spoke in the House only once. Another was given to Chris Wall, Ahern's own election agent in Dublin Central, who never spoke in the chamber at all. (This is not a reflection on either man: the Seanad only met twice for the remainder of their tenure.)

Nonetheless both remain eligible, for life, for all the perks of Oireachtas membership, including lifetime access to Leinster House and its car parks, and indefinite access to the members' bar and restaurant. That is access which, quite literally, money can't buy.

8

TRY IT SOMETIME

Politics is a draining business, but in purely financial terms it is also a rewarding one – provided, of course, you can get elected in the first place.

The tale of Sinéad Gibney is a cautionary example. Having already been a Social Democrat and contested the local elections in Blackrock in 2019, coming close to claiming the final seat, she was all set to contest the 2020 general election until she was made head of the Irish Human Rights and Equality Commission, a job she resigned from in 2024 in order to have a tilt at the European Parliament.

Winning the title of MEP was always a long shot, in particular for a relatively young party and a candidate who had never held public office before. But the point of the exercise was not so much to win as to soften the ground for another attempt: a general election was brewing and Gibney would be a more electable prospect for a seat in Dáil Éireann if she was seen as faring well in a European contest.

Running two elections in quick succession is expensive business, with parties putting up some of their own money – and that of any donors – on the expectation that the candidate will also empty their pockets in pursuit of the prize. European elections have a spending limit of €230,000 per candidate, though only the biggest parties ever come close to spending that much, and Dáil candidates may spend close to €45,000 depending on how big their constituency is. Crucially, however, in an effort to reduce the inhibitions of would-be candidates, the Irish electoral system reimburses the expenses of some candidates, even if they lose. A 'quota' is the minimum number of votes needed under Ireland's electoral system to guarantee success; a candidate who eventually reaches a quarter of a quota, including transfers from other candidates, can reclaim some of the money spent on the campaign. In European elections, that amount is €64,400 – an ideal amount for Gibney and the Social Democrats to therefore consider spending. A reasonable performance – tantamount to getting 5 per cent of the votes in Dublin, as a candidate for a major opposition party – would mean getting the full budget returned and leaving a strengthened candidate for the next run out.

Small parties, however, are not exactly made of money. Public rules dictate that the state funding given to political parties cannot be spent on election campaigns. The party was able to commit €25,000 to Gibney's European run; alongside that, she raised around €15,000 from donors and ploughed in €20,000 of her own money. A good chunk of the latter came from the proceeds of Gibney selling her car.

But when it came to crunch time in the RDS as the European votes were counted in 2024, fortune was against her. With 376,720 valid ballot papers cast, the magic number needed to recoup the election spending was 18,836. Gibney won 16,319 first preferences but failed to pick up enough transfers and was eliminated on the fifteenth count with 18,396. She was 440 votes away from getting the money back and being able to take a running start at a general election campaign. Instead, Gibney was left with all her savings spent, a donor network that would struggle to cough up a second sizeable amount so quickly after the first, no car, and no job.

Thankfully, in the long run, the increased name recognition might have been worth it – Gibney unexpectedly took the fourth and final seat in the Dublin Rathdown constituency five months later, and finished the year as a TD. Financially speaking, however, her Dáil run would have been better served had she never run in the European election at all.

𝄞

Unlike in the United States, where candidates and their surrogate 'political action committees' can spend an infinite amount of cash on trying to secure public office, Ireland has relatively rigid limits on electoral spending. Indirect third-party support is not permitted at all – a donation of any kind, even non-monetary, by a third party has to be treated as a donation to the campaign centrally. (This caused no end of bother for Paschal Donohoe in 2023, after it emerged that a businessman in his constituency had arranged for his own staff to put up Donohoe's election posters. The original electoral paperwork omitted this, acting as if it were a pro-bono donation of labour, but such a donation must still be treated as being worth the equivalent of the workers' wages.)

There are also stipulated limits on how much money a candidate can receive in donations in any given year. No politician can take any more than €1,000 from any one donor in a single year; any donation of €600 or higher must be itemised in an annual donations statement, which is published; no unregistered corporate donor can give anything more than €200; cash donations over €200 must be refused; and anonymous donations are capped at €100. No individual donor, irrespective of how many candidates and parties they're trying to spin, can give donations of more than €1,500 a year.

But it is plainly evident that, within all of those rules, there is scope for workaround and outright evasion. Though the likes of a donations bucket left outside Sunday Mass is no longer fashionable, the principle still allows for cash donations to be made under a veil of anonymity. It is relatively common for a TD to declare a few hundred euro of cash donations as part of their annual disclosure to the Standards in Public Office Commission (SIPO), and label them as the aggregate total of multiple donations that cannot be disaggregated or linked to specific individuals. A race night or some other local fundraiser is easy fodder for cash in a bucket.

The perception of transparency is just that: a perception. While politicians are required to send bank statements to SIPO as part of their disclosures process – and politicians will routinely expect some over-and-back querying elements of their paperwork – these bank statements are not published. Nor are they released as part of any Freedom of Information request: they are withheld on the premise that publication would involve compromising personal details of third parties. The only element that will ever see the light of day is the cover page, on which a politician ticks a box about whether any €600+ donations were made and lists the names of any such donors. Any number of hypothetical donors could offer €599.99 in donations each year and never have that detail published.

Ω

The other gaping hole in the rules about money in politics concerns spending, specifically spending around elections.

The rules on donations are blind to the timing of elections, which – for those who would like to avoid politicians buying influence – is an undoubtedly positive development. The scheduling of a public vote has no impact on the amount candidates might be able to take from supportive benefactors, so while election years are infinitely more expensive, there is no fast-track way to get extra money in the door.

The rules on spending are relatively straightforward in principle: depending on the population of the area being represented (at council level) or the number of people being elected (for the Dáil) there are straightforward limits on how much you are allowed to spend within the election period.

But there are plenty of ways to beat the clock on election spending by simply spending money *before* the election is made official. For local and European elections this is particularly routine: the world already knows there will be elections in late May or early June of 2029, and of 2034, and 2039, and so on. The law, however, cannot be in 'election mode' forever: a rule preventing public representatives from advertising in newspapers wouldn't be practicable at non-election times if a TD or councillor is simply trying to advertise the times of constituency clinics, or even to publicise their contact details. The clock therefore only begins ticking on electoral expenses 60 days before the election is due: if voting takes place in the first week of June, the spending rules will only kick in from around the first week of April.

This transparency allows politicians to flog themselves into the ground, paying for billboards in town centres, or displays beside major motorways, incurring costs that are far beyond what could be sanctioned during a campaign. Leaflets that are printed up in late March, which don't make any overt mention of an election and merely hint-hint-nudge-nudge at a forthcoming trip to the ballot box, could be sent to homes over the next two months with no consequence on electoral spending rules.

If you've ever found a pamphlet in your letterbox from a politician who has cut a distant figure in the previous few years, and whose re-election is approaching, now you know why: it's not just that the election is coming, but that sending it early enough means the cost of printing doesn't count as an electoral expense.

The argument for pamphleteering is even greater for members of the Dáil and Seanad, who have their own in-house printing service in Leinster House. (Regular followers of national media will remember this one: the current industrial printing press was purchased with the intention of being placed in a mismeasured room that wasn't big enough to house it safely, and remedial structural works costing over €230,000 were needed to squeeze it in.) While notionally intended to provide representatives with letterheaded A4 paper and other basic items of stationery, the service has expanded over time, and politicians will often commission all sorts of gimmicky jobs to spread their faces and buy a little more name recognition. Michael Healy-Rae in Kerry is a master of the simple job of distributing household calendars with bank holidays and other national events pre-slotted in – alongside photographs of the man himself hard at work, and contact details for his offices. Others prefer to piggyback on sporting events: Fine Gael's Neale Richmond has previously distributed personalised wallcharts highlighting fixtures in the Rugby World Cup, including games in which Ireland would feature. His party colleague Noel Rock, an aficionado of the round ball, issued similar calendars to households in Dublin North-West after his election with the fixture details for Euro 2016. Other TDs admitted to being a little annoyed they hadn't thought of the idea first: Rock's calendars also did the rounds within Leinster House, circulated by parliamentarians trying to brainstorm similar ideas for novelty wares. (This was not entirely without a snag: the Oireachtas originally refused to produce them, unconvinced of the merits for the constituents of Dublin North-West, but relented when the design was adjusted so that the back page of the calendar would include details on how to apply for sports capital grants.)

The hardest rule precluding some uses of the Oireachtas printing facility is that explicitly electoral messages cannot be facilitated, and so marginally more oblique language is needed. Deputy Joe Bloggs cannot ask for a calendar that asks constituents to 'Vote Bloggs Number 1!', but can certainly procure leaflets highlighting all his important contributions alongside a reminder that he is 'Your Local Voice Working Hard In Dáil Éireann'. In an industry where name recognition is currency, it's an easy way to plant a seed in a voter's mind.

Dáil elections differ from others in their timing. Sometimes a general election will be called at short notice by a taoiseach who thinks the timing is opportune, either striking at a moment of swelling popularity or opting to cut and run before matters turn irrevocably sour. But in other instances it is plainly obvious when TDs will be up for re-election: if the outgoing taoiseach explicitly declares they want their cabinet to serve its maximum possible term, deputies can be relatively assured that the next election will be five years after the last one. This, combined with the fact that the 60-day spending rule cannot apply until an election has been called, allows candidates to frontload their electoral spending – this can be done either by using the Leinster House printing service or splashing out on billboards and other showy displays of power ahead of time.

Candidacy is expensive. One TD in an urban constituency with a relatively small footprint reckons you need about €15,000 to be able to mount a realistic challenge for a seat. That estimate applies for a member of a political party that can negotiate a better national rate for printing posters or election materials. Independent candidates in built-up areas can find their spending coming to almost €30,000. Even at scale, a single election poster printed on durable Corriboard costs about €6 – and if there aren't enough volunteers to mount those posters afterward, most commercial agencies will charge about €1.50 to mount each one. Throw in the expectation of sorting out volunteers too – covering the costs of filling their cars, receipts for minibus and taxi journeys, a tray of sandwiches at the end of an evening's canvass – and other ancillary costs like adverts in the local newspaper, and the costs can soon mount up.

𝄞

There is one class of election, however, in which there is no spending limit. Elections to the Seanad do not have any ceiling on the amount a candidate can spend on their campaign, and while senators themselves are still subject to the same limits on donations, their campaigns can spend an infinitely deep pool of cash in pursuit of a seat in Leinster House's lesser chamber.

Part of the reason for this is the fact that senators can be elected (or appointed) in three different ways. As described in Chapter 7, six are chosen by graduates of the country's universities; 43 are elected through vocational panels, where the only voters are TDs, councillors and outgoing senators themselves; and 11 are appointed by whoever emerges as taoiseach following a general election as an inevitable act of inter-coalition bartering. It would be foolhardy, if not outright impossible, to try and stipulate a single spending limit for campaigns with such different dynamics.

That, at least, is the official explanation. A more informal theory around Leinster House is that laws adopted in 2012 to update the political spending regime never considered including the Seanad, simply because the government was planning for its abolition. A referendum in October 2013 to scrap the upper house entirely was defeated by 52 per cent to 48. The prevailing presumption among long-standing senators is that a cap on campaign spending, which could have been feasible if the different constituencies had different limits, was simply overlooked on the presumption that the Seanad wouldn't exist by the time of the next election anyway.

When it comes to the vocational panels, which fill 43 of the Seanad's 60 seats, there is no need for tallies or for detailed psephological analysis of the electorate: unlike in a Dáil election, the party affiliation of every single voter is already known. This has the effect of both streamlining the election – a Fianna Fáil candidate, for example, need only canvass fellow party members – and making it an inadvertent bidding war.

Sinn Féin is ordinarily disciplined enough to manage its vote in the Seanad with precision, so it will decide centrally which one or two candidates will put their names forward and maximise their chance of success on any given panel. The other parties are a little more tolerant of personal ambition, however, and it is common for some candidates to be favoured by party headquarters while others mount solo efforts to get elected. This runs the risk of splitting the vote: there might be enough Fianna Fáil votes to take 4 seats out of 11 on one panel, but there might be so many candidates vying for victory that the vote is spread too thinly between them. In 2020, the Fine Gael electorate may have been big enough to take three seats out of nine on the Industrial and Commercial Panel, but no fewer than 16 candidates put their names forward.

How does one stand apart from the crowd? For a long time, Seanad elections effectively became auctions. The electorate for vocational panels is so small that any aspiring candidate is expected to hit the road and press the flesh with as many of the voters as possible. Candidates speak of being on the road for a week or two at a time, spending a precious few hours a night in provincial hotel beds, converting the side roads of Ireland into an Eulerian circuit of councillors' homes. There are war stories about candidates getting delayed on a journey, showing up at a councillor's home after the family had gone to bed, and apologetically waking them up simply to stop the councillor feeling they had been snubbed. It is doubtful that many electors will think positively of the candidate who woke up the kids in the course of a canvass.

But it is not enough to simply show up and tell someone what you'll bring to the role. A common practice is to bring some kind of token or trinket, to be left ostensibly as a keepsake, and effectively as an auxiliary bribe. Bottles of wine or whiskey are common; if the election is due early in a year, canvassing over Christmas might entail a nice hamper being delivered to a few select supporters. Senators shiver in fear at a Dáil election being called in the final months of the year: Seanad elections follow within 90 days of a general election, prompting a lot of festive driving.

Some are able to offer more niche gifts: Fianna Fáil three-term senator Mary White was also the co-founder of Lir Chocolates and was able to leave a slightly sweeter keepsake for would-be supporters. Her party colleague Donie Cassidy, a showband saxophonist who then became a music publisher and promoter, was reputed to have a car boot full of CDs produced by his best-known act, Foster and Allen, to be left as souvenirs of a canvassing visit. ('I wonder did he realise', says one uncharitable analyst, 'that the boys were going out of fashion in 2011 and that there was no point running in the election that year?')

More recently, Gerard Craughwell – who, as an independent, has to cast the net for votes more widely than others – sent enamel lapel pins, featuring the crest of each councillor's respective county, to all 949 members of the city and county councils.

For aspiring senators, the downside is that none of the expense of a Seanad election can be recouped – even a victorious senator won't get any of their money back at the end of the race. But for those who are minded to sink their time and money into a candidacy, the opportunity is there to run a high-profile and expensive campaign that might well yield a seat as a member of the Irish parliament. Elections for the six university seats, where the electorate is so wide as to garner a small amount of media coverage, are low-hanging fruit. The only things stopping a university candidate from taking out a nationwide billboard or newspaper advertising campaign, flooding every letterbox with promotional material and turning themselves into the highest-profile candidate possible, are time and money. A candidate with both could, almost literally, buy their way into Leinster House.

⚷

Once they are ensconced in office, it might be perceived that politicians are all on the gravy train. The jobs come with decent salaries – six figures for TDs, even more in a ministry, with tens of thousands a year in extra allowances.

The truth is a little more complicated. Yes, the wages are excellent – and it is undoubtedly true that the lion's share of ordinary workers do not get to claim expenses for the very act of driving to work in the first place. Indeed, almost all politicians will respectfully stop short of making any kind of on-the-record critique of the system. Nobody on a six-figure salary, in a job whose security depends on public satisfaction, wants to raise their head above the parapet and complain about the allowances.

Ultimately, they all have the memory of Pádraig Flynn's immortal appearance on *The Late Late Show* in 1999, which included a dispassionate lament on his cost of living as Ireland's EU commissioner. 'Give or take, it works out at about – with expenses – a hundred and forty thousand [pounds] a year, and I pay thirty point three per cent tax on that, so it's about a net hundred thousand; and out of that hundred thousand I run a home in Dublin, Castlebar and Brussels. I wanna tell you something: try it sometime, when you've a couple of cars and three houses […] and a few housekeepers …'

The unspeakable truth for politicians is that, despite the public anger that followed Flynn's somewhat tone-deaf comment, Flynn was correct and the cost of a political life can often be higher than the wage that comes with it.

Take for example the perception that TDs and senators receive healthy pay top-ups through the Leinster House expenses regime. This view is fuelled by occasional news reports outlining how much in 'expenses' has been paid to politicians in the month of August, when the Dáil and Seanad almost never sit. (The author humbly admits to his own small role in this: in previous jobs, without having gained a nuanced understanding of the system, he has authored pieces about the hundreds of thousands being 'claimed' by politicians who aren't actually at work at all in the month of August.)

The misunderstanding here is that politicians don't receive 'expenses' in the same way that most employees would understand them, where costs are incurred and receipts are submitted afterwards. Rather, politicians are entitled to various *allowances* which are paid upfront and can be used to meet certain costs related to their duties. The two primary allowances are simply paid in 12 equal monthly instalments, which are routinely published by the Oireachtas in a notional act of transparency which actually achieves very little. So it is not merely the case that a politician 'got a few thousand in expenses for a month that they weren't working' – it's actually that they got their regular payment of a sum that goes to covering the costs of their year-round duties.

When granted anonymity, members are frank about how difficult it can be to make those allowances stretch to cover the job. Those in rural constituencies – in particular those that cover an entire county, or sometimes multiple counties – are routinely expected to have a bigger presence on the ground than the allowances would envisage.

One TD in a whole-county constituency breaks it down thusly. The salary of a TD is about €113,000 but the take-home pay, after the regular income taxes, public service levy, a contribution to the Oireachtas health insurance scheme and a separate pension contribution, comes to a little over €4,400 per month. A TD based outside Leinster can expect about €30,000 a year in the Travel and Accommodation Allowance (TAA) – all of which they will use, given the costs incurred not only travelling to and from Dublin, and staying in hotels in the capital for sitting nights, but also circulating within the constituency (and potentially beyond, if the TD concerned is a prominent figure in an opposition party). This allowance is graded, depending on the mileage of the commute from Leinster House to the politician's home. Those with the longest commutes from the tips of Cork can get over €34,000 a year on the TAA; those within 25km of the capital get the 'Dublin' rate of €9,000, working out at €750 a month. Some politicians have been known to take liberties with this, claiming that the quickest route to Leinster House is not always the shortest one. It's a distinction worth making: the difference between a 24.9km commute and a 25.1km commute is €1,358 per month, or roughly €113 for each day that the Dáil actually sits.

Then there's a separate annual Public Representation Allowance (PRA), a flat rate of €20,350, which is supposed to cover the cost of running a constituency presence – floor space, utilities, stationery, phone bills, webspace, venue rental, ads in the local papers, leaflet distribution. Even the most modest office space, with an outer waiting area and an inner office, would eat up most of that budget. Multiply it by two, if you're trying to keep a presence in two major towns in the constituency, and the costs start to mount. And who will staff those two offices? The TD's administrative assistant might typically be asked to stay back in the constituency but can only hold the fort in one office at a time, so someone else has to be recruited on part-time hours for the second office. Suddenly the €4,400-ish in monthly take-home pay for the TD doesn't stretch very far, especially if they've got younger mouths to feed at home.

The allowances 'make a lot of sense in terms of ensuring democracy is democratic', says Patrick Costello of the Green Party. 'They make sure that being a TD is open to all, because that's the important thing.' His view is that if the allowances did not exist, running the likes of a constituency office would simply be unviable for all but the richest of deputies. 'We have this for a reason – so you can ensure a cross-section of society is there.'

It is for this reason that a junior ministry was once more of a financial curse than a blessing. While promotion to ministerial ranks is obviously a stepping stone to higher office, the consequences for a new appointee's bank account could be significant. Appointment as a minister of state means an increase in pay of close to €46,000 – hardly to be sniffed at. But, until 2025, the consequence of promotion was that parliamentary allowances were deducted: the PRA for running a constituency office was cut by over €4,000, and the travel allowance was scrapped completely, on the presumption that departments would cover travel costs instead. TDs from farther afield, who would have been receiving larger travel allowances because of the length of their commutes to Leinster House, thus found themselves out of pocket by taking on the higher duties.

One interviewee for this book confirmed they materially lost money in getting promoted, given the extent of the travel involved in the brief to which they were assigned. While cabinet-level ministers are provided with luxury garda-driven vehicles for transport ('Mercs and perks', as they're casually labelled, although as a matter of fact most of the cars are now Audis), junior ministers are provided with drivers but have to provide their own cars and retroactively claim mileage that might only just cover the depreciating value of the vehicles. Many a minister – including most of those of cabinet grade, who were not provided with Garda cars from 2011 until a security review in 2022 – has bought a new car to mark their appointment and found it almost worthless by the time they left, given the sheer amount of travel entailed in the job.

While the mileage expenses they incur are ordinarily covered by their department, a minister's accommodation costs are not always recoupable. This is because a junior minister's extra profile entails having to do more for the party: they will regularly be asked to attend party events in opposite corners of the country, perhaps presiding over constituency conventions, or attending public meetings as a guest of some up-and-coming councillor who wants to build a local profile ahead of the next election. In those circumstances, the department (naturally) will not foot the bill for accommodation, and the new minister will either have to stump up for their own lodgings or ask the driver to bring them home at all hours to get a few broken hours of compromised sleep.

The financial gap between backbencher and low-level minister is even more acute if the TD had previously been holding down a second job alongside their life in Leinster House. The vast majority of politicians do not do this, and those who arrive particularly young generally don't have time to develop and pursue a side career afterward. However, it remains relatively common for the likes of GPs, shopkeepers, solicitors or barristers to win seats in Dáil Éireann and to try and perform both roles at once, especially given the profile afforded by those older jobs might be the very reason they got elected in the first place. A politician with a busy commercial premises might be able to spend Mondays or Fridays in their 'old' job, in particular if it's a public-facing business where constituents might come in and have an opportunity to meet their local TD, with the premises doubling up as an auxiliary constituency office.

Ministers of state, however, have no such flexibility, and are often roped into their departments on Mondays to attend to various executive functions, having only some Fridays of their own for local work. For those in the medical or legal professions, there is even a risk of going out of business outright; solicitors and larger-scale GPs might be able to leave their practices in the hands of partners, but barristers (who are self-employed) can only hope to garner an income in the Law Library if they are actually available to take instructions and present a client's case in court. If the whole point of being a barrister is having the right of audience in a courtroom, there is no money to be made by being elsewhere.

There is at least one case where somebody is suspected of voluntarily giving up a ministerial career because of this financial consequence: the salary increase was roughly on par with the allowances lost, but the scant availability to work at the 'day job' meant the politician was significantly worse off overall. The title was higher, but the wallet lighter.

$$\Omega$$

An element of political life not budgeted for – literally – is when politicians find themselves in the courts looking to vindicate a political position. There are a few examples of it: Pearse Doherty, then a senator, took a successful challenge in 2010 after a vacant seat in his constituency had been left idle for well over a year. Pat 'the Cope' Gallagher had become an MEP, but in the midst of ongoing recession and fiscal turmoil, the government had little appetite for any unnecessary electoral tests. Doherty was left to pursue action in the High Court before winning a judgment requiring the seat to be filled. He won the ensuing by-election, and has been a TD ever since.

Others have not had the same measure of success. Catherine Murphy and Finian McGrath made an unsuccessful complaint that the election of May 2007 didn't take account of the preliminary result of the previous year's census, which would have prescribed the addition of extra seats to Dáil Éireann. Independent TD Thomas Pringle lost a 2012 case arguing that a European bailout mechanism was a breach of the EU's founding treaties. The socialist deputy Joan Collins had a related case, also unsuccessful, about state assistance to two bailed-out banks and the need for Dáil approval first.

There was one silver lining to those cases; in each instance the courts determined that the challenges brought by the deputies were of significant public importance, such that each would be able to have their costs paid by the state. Such clarity is welcome: otherwise, the general rule in legal cases is that costs 'follow the award' and that the loser must pay not only their own legal costs, but also those of the state. There are no Oireachtas allowances to help TDs take cases against the state or its agencies: without the exceptional treatment of the courts, those politicians would have been on the hook for enormous costs.

It is even rarer again for a government TD to find themselves suing their own government. Such was the position of the Greens' Patrick Costello, however, over coalition plans to ratify an EU trade deal with Canada. Leo Varadkar, as enterprise minister, was keen to have the deal approved, and ensured that a reference to its ratification was enshrined in the Programme for Government. Costello, however, was especially aggrieved at the role of investor courts within the deal, which in principle opened the door for companies to sue any government that introduced laws that might constrain their ability to turn a profit.

'Any time we've created new courts, we've done so by way of constitutional amendment,' Costello explains. 'Ratifying the International Criminal Court, the Court of Appeal, signing up to the Courts of Justice of the European Union, always took a constitutional referendum. I found myself just arguing that point, and being focused on "How do they get around Crotty?" Crotty being the decision about how we need a referendum on all our EU treaties.

'I texted a couple of barristers I know, and said it to them: "How do you get around Crotty?" And one of them just replied to me and said, "They don't."'

The argument was brought up at the Greens' parliamentary party meetings, with limited sympathy for his case. Some saw ratifying the deal as the price of power-sharing – you win policy concessions in some areas but have to back down in others. Others saw the concern as overstated, given all trade deals include some kind of mechanism for resolving disputes. Costello, on both a policy and a legal standpoint, told the party leadership he could not vote for it.

'The thing was,' Costello says, 'it was permanent. We've passed bills that I have constitutional questions over, but they're not permanent: there's still the possibility of a remedy in the courts. The problem with this was that it became this vast international thing that we'd never be able to leave. We'd have to leave the European Union to be able to leave CETA if it passed, and I don't want that! The permanence of it had me driven to a place where we'd have got to look at this in a much more serious way.'

Weighing up a legal case had a lot of considerations. There were the straightforward optics of a TD taking a case against a government where his own party held office. There was the possibility of stirring up anti-EU contrarianism, which Costello himself did not subscribe to.

But underlying all of this was the question of costs. Barristers had advised him that his case would 'more than likely' fall within similar categories to the likes of Pringle's and Collins's, being of such public importance that the state would be told to cover his costs. 'But it was never a guarantee, it was a "more than likely". Yes, there is strong precedent, but every case turns on its own merits, and the judge might have decided there was something different about my case versus Pringle or versus Collins. The barristers did agree to work on a contingency, a "no foal, no fee" basis, but they could have left stung and not been paid for two years' work … you couldn't rule it out.'

And that meant big questions about the possible consequences if the case did not go his way. 'There was a lot of talk about, what are the risks here, how much is this going to cost if we lose? Are we going to have to remortgage the house? Are we going to have to sell the house? What the hell do we do? How do we manage this if the worst came to the worst?'

The High Court found against Costello's case, believing there was no contradiction between the deal and the constitution – and only awarding Costello half of his own costs. The judge effectively found that, as a serving TD who could reap political benefit from being associated with the case, he would have to bear some costs himself. There was nothing for it: it would have to be appealed further, the stakes raised. Double or nothing.

In November 2022 a majority of the Supreme Court eventually found in his favour: while the problems might have been overcome with a change in domestic law, the EU–Canada deal in its original form would have been unconstitutional and required a referendum to approve. Costello's victory meant the topic became so thorny that the government of the day refused to touch it for the remainder of its tenure. The decision in his favour also meant the entire costs incurred by Costello, from the High Court upwards, would be covered by the state.

'In weighing it up, it was, what are the consequences of this case not being taken, and what is the risk, versus, what is the risk of going ahead? There would still have been quite a risk, but at the end of the day, it was a risk that needed to be taken. The fact that the [Supreme] Court found in my favour highlights that I was right!'

Plenty of coalition TDs might have grievances with the activities of their own government, and even try to take a fight to their ministerial colleagues, but there are no others who have – literally – bet their house on it.

ƍ

'The pension is excellent,' one serving TD says. 'There's no getting away from that: if you're lucky enough to do twenty years in Leinster House, you get the full pension and that's a real comfort for future years. But if people think that this is a job where you get rich, they're absolutely wrong.'

This view is reflected across the board in Leinster House – at least, among those who are not blessed with the extra €92,000 wage of a full cabinet minister. 'The lived experience for a Dublin TD,' says one such metropolitan,' is about four and a half thousand a month after tax and pension deductions. It's a good wage, don't get me wrong. But it's not nearly as exorbitant as outsiders think.'

One particular grievance is the perception that the pension system is particularly gilded. It certainly has its upsides compared to other pension systems: parliamentarians qualify for the full pension after 20 years of service, compared to civil servants, who have to clock up 40 years of contributions before qualifying. But reforms introduced in the wake of the 2010 financial crisis mean it's no longer an immediate payout when members leave. Now a member first elected after 2011 must turn 65 before accessing the first payments. 'There's a complete misapprehension out there that newly elected TDs could retire in their forties and fifties,' says one more recent parliamentarian. 'There's no such thing. Even if you happened to get in at age thirty, and left at age fifty, you'd have qualified for the full pension but you wouldn't get near it for another fifteen years.'

In addition, one oft-overlooked aspect of the pension system is that politicians themselves pay a huge chunk of the pension cost. Those who clock up 20 years of service in the job get an annual pension equivalent to half a TD's wage; those leaving now on a full pension would get about €57,000 a year, a self-evidently handsome annual payment for someone who no longer needs to make any contribution to public life. Less well known, however, is the fact that TDs make much bigger contributions to their eventual pension pots than most others. The pension contribution is not paid in addition to the salary; it forms part of it. A full 19.9 per cent of a deputy's gross pay is kept aside for eventual pension contributions.

'The first time I got a payslip, I was like, there's a quarter of it missing!', says one TD. 'I thought I was paying emergency tax or something. So I rang them up. "Oh, no, that's your pension."

'Yeah, we get a nice pension out of it at the end, but you're paying for it now. But you won't get any sympathy because yeah, the pension, or the golden parachute [of severance payments] or whatever.'

Another takes issue with occasional surveys run by newspapers, which seek to calculate the wealth of every member of the Dáil. James O'Connor, the Fianna Fáil TD for Cork East who was first elected age 22, featured highly on one list – solely on the basis that because of his young age, and the fact he would be set to receive pension payments in four decades' time, the actuarial value of his pension pot was statistically high.

Another aspect of this issue is that, owing to the high pensions that are linked to their specific jobs, politicians (like judges) pay a different type of PRSI to most. Class K contributions do not count towards the contributory state pension, nor towards other things like eye tests. Councillors, who get annual pay and allowances of about €31,000 but no pension, are materially worse off.

Publicly, politicians naturally do not complain about this. The median wage for the average full-time worker in Ireland is in the region of €46,000; a TD's take-home pay is higher than the gross pay of their average constituent. But it is not as cosseted as most presume.

'If someone looked at my bank balance now,' says one TD ruefully, 'they'd probably think I had a gambling problem. They'd wonder where the hell all the money had gone to.'

9

NEVER AT HOME

'We spend a lot of time in our cars,' says one TD. 'Our cars, or at desks, or in function rooms. I think I put on about a stone in my first eighteen months.'

Politicians get this a lot. There are naturally the long working hours, sometimes necessitating eating on the go and continual snacking, especially in cars in between appointments. Then there's the relatively sedentary style of working: the long periods spent behind a steering wheel, or sitting at desks in committee rooms: there are a few stories of people who believed themselves to be getting exercise by having to continually walk from one spot in Leinster House to another, then getting new Apple Watches or Fitbits and realising they often spent two or three hours in a single chair without even standing up for as much as a toilet break.

Then there is the self-service canteen, the home of a cost-price lunchtime carvery dinner, and the same again at teatime. Quite a few staff in Leinster House, both political and civilian, admit to getting into a bad habit of eating dinner at lunchtime (who could resist a meat-and-two-veg main course for around €6.50?), knowing they might make it home for dinnertime later, only to revisit the canteen later that evening and end up having a second dinner there. Earlier arrivals can also avail of the cut-price breakfast; a Full Irish in the canteen, including tea or coffee, costs little more than a fiver. 'You go in with the best of intentions, telling yourself you're going to have granola, and then you see the rashers and sausages all lined up ...' laments one politician.

There is a built-in facility designed to address these health concerns: a fully furnished gym in the basement floor of an Oireachtas office block across the road on Kildare Street, complete with a personal trainer who can help politicians (and non-politicians) to build a fitness regime that keeps them in fighting shape. The downside is the inevitable encounters between parliamentary colleagues in the changing room.

'I went in there to do a session,' says one. 'Nice facility, the trainer showed me what they had; did some lifts, was fairly happy, was going to try and make this into a routine … I go back into the changing room and sit down, and up comes another TD who's getting changed for his own workout, and who says hello to me … totally bollock naked.

'Nothing could put me off going to the gym any quicker than the thought of ending up at eye level with another TD's bollocks.'

𝛺

Aside from the long hours of the Dáil itself, the duties of a TD are so manifold that the work can never truly be declared 'done'. There might always be someone looking for help on one front or another, and the phone can never truly be turned off.

When Leo Varadkar first became a TD in 2007, he received a note of counsel from the former Labour leader Ruairi Quinn. Quinn was 60, and 30 years into a full-time political career; Varadkar was 28 and was only just becoming full-time himself, having previously juggled a county council seat with his pursuit of medicine. Quinn recognised Varadkar's enthusiasm but warned him to hold a little in reserve. Politics is full on, Quinn said: if you don't schedule free time, you won't have any – and if you're going to last 20–30 years, you ought to get into that habit. Better to aspire to make an appointment than to leave it to chance and fail.

Another nugget of wisdom received by one TD was, when they became a councillor for the first time, to get a second mobile phone with a new number for work purposes. To them, this was counterintuitive: they had got elected based on their presence in their community and their contactability, and surely they'd need to remain in touch with the people who put them in the job? No, said the older figure: get out ahead of the problem now. If you ever become a TD, people will expect you to keep the same number you had as a councillor, and if that's still your personal number, you'll never be able to turn your phone off.

It's a lesson others have taken into the job. One particularly savvy TD has a phone with two SIM card slots – one personal, one professional – which not only allows the work number to be activated as the need arises, but also means WhatsApp can only ever operate on one number (their personal one). Not having WhatsApp, they find, allows a certain degree of headspace – such is the ubiquity of that instant messaging app that not having a presence there tends to inhibit people from bombarding them with inquiries.

'Oh,' says another, when the idea of having two separate phones is mentioned to them. 'I wish I'd thought of that. It'd be nice to be able to keep up with the family group chat.'

Others can see the upside. The work is so all-consuming for full-time politicians that keeping a single number, complete with WhatsApp groups, is a lifeline to the 'real' world.

'You might meet a couple of friends for dinner or something, and you realise it's been fourteen or fifteen months since you last did it with them,' says Labour's Duncan Smith. 'WhatsApp groups are a lifesaver for my relationships with my friends – you know, just being able to be in ongoing conversations about football, or wrestling, or whatever. I find that really important to me, because I may not get to be face to face with them, but I feel I'm still in a kind of daily contact. I still might not know what's going on – they might have got a new job or something, that's not the content! But they're [the texts] something I can absorb in the walk from the car to the desk. I can have ninety seconds of time with my friends. I don't think they realise how important that is to me.'

ঃ

Escape valves like that are enormously important as a method of release. Even those who go into the job after periods on local authorities can find it all-encompassing and uncomfortably impinging on their personal lives.

'I am very lucky,' says Louise O'Reilly of Sinn Féin, for whom the role of a TD has parallels with the ebb and flow of her previous job as a trade union official working in industrial relations. 'For the last twenty-odd years I've had a job like this – my other job was a little bit like this, because you're dealing with people, and you'd be down at the Labour Court, you're looking like you might get a resolution, [and] you're thinking, "I'm not gonna leave it here if we're going to get this resolved," so you're ringing your husband and going, "I understand it's my turn to do the dinner, my turn to do everything else … [but] sorry about that, I won't be home this evening. You will have to take over." I had that in my previous job. By the time I got elected [in 2016], my daughter was grown up, moved out and had a child of her own, so I didn't have any of that at home.

'Now, in saying that, I am actually very fond of my husband! And I do enjoy spending time with him, so I miss being able to say definitively [we'll do something], and schedule time.'

The approach taken by O'Reilly echoes Ruairi Quinn's warning to Leo Varadkar. The evening O'Reilly was interviewed for this book, she had tickets to see the West End production of the smash hit musical *Hamilton*, which was in residence at the Bord Gáis Energy Theatre. 'We booked it for a Thursday night, because on Friday I do my clinics, and I never want to do anything on a Friday night, because I'm exhausted – I'm absolutely wiped, and you wouldn't be in the mood to go somewhere nice. I generally go home and just get into the bath, and try to get my head straight, because [in the job] you see a lot of people who are in very bad circumstances.'

But everything is contingent. O'Reilly's husband also has certain inflexibilities in his job, and it can be hard to arrange a day on which both can set aside a few hours – and even those arrangements can fall by the wayside at short notice because of the nature of her work. As a frontbench spokesperson, she must always be prepared to drop everything and attend to an urgent crisis. As enterprise spokesperson, for example, O'Reilly might learn of major redundancies being planned at a multinational, and go to meet employee representatives, or appear on TV news bulletins outlining what might be needed in a government response. If the call comes from *Prime Time* asking to appear on a panel, the *Hamilton* tickets – bought over a year in advance – simply get passed on to someone else.

If those are the challenges faced by prominent figures in opposition, cabinet ministers have even more demands. All are expected to maintain some presence in their constituencies, while also being in Dublin for cabinet on Tuesdays, remaining around Dublin on Wednesdays, and possibly spending the rest of the week on the road. Heather Humphreys' third stint in cabinet entailed two roles, juggling both the high-spending Department of Social Protection – and big reforms like auto-enrolment for pensions, or linking post-redundancy benefits to workers' existing salaries – and the Department of Rural and Community Development, which involved an intense travel schedule and usually meant every Saturday was spent on the road far from home.

The only thing that made the lifestyle manageable was the fact that Humphreys' two children were already 21 and 18 by the time of her first election to Dáil Éireann. Juggling a part-time role as a county councillor with her full-time credit union job had been difficult enough; in national politics she tried to ringfence Mondays as a constituency day ('the nature of politics is you cannot stop, because if you stop, somebody else passes you out, especially when it comes to the constituency') and there simply wasn't much time left to do anything else. 'On a Sunday, I always liked a bit of gardening,' she ventures. 'Maybe cook a dinner for the girls.' The draining lifestyle of a full-time minister, she suggested, was the primary reason the job couldn't be sustained.

Another TD puts it more simply. 'Between one election and the next, you're never not a TD. All hours, day or night. If people have a problem, you'll be one of the first people they think of calling.'

🔑

One of the first episodes of *The West Wing*, the celebrated TV drama depicting the working lives of senior officials in the White House, paints a picture that some politicians can empathise with. Leo McGarry, the resilient and unflappable chief of staff, arrives home at 2 a.m. after a challenging day trying to rescue a failing bill on gun control. He finds an abandoned candlelit dinner going cold on the table, and his wife, Jenny, standing deflated on the staircase. He has forgotten their wedding anniversary, and is evidently struggling to maintain any kind of family life.

'This is the most important thing I'll ever do, Jenny. I have to do it well,' McGarry plaintively tells his wife.

'It's not more important than your marriage,' she replies.

'It is more important than my marriage right now,' he announces, as if the decision is crystallising in his mind in real time. 'These few years while I'm doing this: yes, it's more important than my marriage.'

It is a scene with which many in Leinster House can empathise. An underreported aspect of life for Irish politicians is that, while some meet the love of their life when working in close quarters with a handful of others, there is also a relatively high proportion of relationship breakdown.

This is naturally a sensitive and discreet area, so much so that the author has chosen not to ask direct questions of those who are known to have gone through the process. Those in similar lines of work, however – no matter their political allegiance – can empathise with how the demands of the job, and the desire to do it well, can preoccupy a TD or senator so much that their partner simply begins to feel more and more of a stranger in their life.

In one instance, the challenge was not trying to stay in touch, but rather managing the stress of the job. One politician who has undergone a relationship breakdown had hired their partner as one of their personal staff, on the original basis that they were a core part of the team that got them elected in the first place, and if the job was to be all-encompassing, it made sense to take it on together. As it turned out, the strain of the job and the infinite workload proved incompatible with their relationship.

One political parent suggests that full-time politicos become so busy with the role that, especially if coming from outside of Dublin, the rearing of the children is a natural point of contention. The partner remaining at home, left to manage the house and look after the children, might reasonably become frustrated with the politician's inability to keep a schedule. So much so that, this parent suggests, it might simply become more reasonable to separate, and formalise an arrangement where the politician is not expected to be around any more.

'I can totally see how it happens,' this parent ventures. 'Totally. Because you have to remember, a lot of people in here have made it their life's work to become a TD. You know? They were political as children, or as teenagers, and have never seen themselves doing anything else. They were married to the job long before they ever met anyone or had kids. They were probably married to the job before they even *had* the job.

'And to be honest: if you really want to feel like you're giving it your all, then by extension, you're almost never at home.'

One politician interviewed for this book, but who asked to remain off the record, is frank. 'The hardest part for me is the impact it has on the amount of time you see your children. It does take you away from a huge amount of things that you miss. I've found that extremely difficult.

'If I had my time over again, would I do it again? I'd have to ask myself that fairly seriously.'

Others, reassuringly, take the opposite view and credit their children for forcing them to take time out and away from the treadmill. People Before Profit's Paul Murphy and his wife, Jess, welcomed baby Juniper in February 2023.

'I'm not a huge fan of being a TD, but since having a child, I've seen there is one positive, which is relative flexibility. You are to some degree your own boss: it is possible for your child to make you take the day off. I've seen positives that I previously wouldn't have.

'Even the time when you start: you don't always *have* to be in at nine o'clock every day. Yes, there are some days you absolutely have to be in, and obviously you're definitely working more than nine to five each day. But it's possible for us to get in for ten o'clock instead, and work from home in the meantime.'

10

GETTING NOTICED

There are a few ways a parliamentarian can try and build up a profile. The first, naturally enough, is to become an active contributor in the Dáil or Seanad.

That is slightly easier said than done. Many people have the image of Dáil debates where a TD can simply put up their hand, speak for a few minutes, and then pass on the baton to somebody else. But debate is never as free-flowing or spontaneous as this: the allocation of speaking time is very carefully stage-managed, which is one of the reasons why the chamber often appears nearly empty (as discussed elsewhere in this book, there is little point in being in the chamber for long stretches of time if you aren't going to have a speaking slot). Speaking time is allotted by the party whips, who will send around a draft agenda for each week's sitting, and leave it up to TDs to enquire about getting some time on a specific debate.

On this front, the early bird catches the worm. Smaller parties or technical groups often have very short allocations of speaking time, and technical groups in particular can be especially difficult to manage, constituted as they are by independent or small-party TDs who are expected to be capable spokespersons on all topics (unlike TDs from major parties who can trust their assigned spokesperson to take the lead on a specific subject). The few precious minutes of speaking time allocated to a technical group might end up being divided into exceptionally thin slices, should every member of a group feel the need to have their say.

There are, however, other ways to go about things. A lottery system allows for four 'Topical Issues' to be raised in the chamber every day, irrespective of the day's predetermined schedule. This can be a godsend for government backbenchers, offering them a public opportunity to question their own ministerial colleagues on their response to, or management of, an important constituency issue. A TD who knows they can gain popularity by visibly demanding more resources for the local hospital, for instance, might regularly try to raise this as a Topical Issue in the hope of pinning down some kind of concession from the minister.

At least, that's how the system is intended to work; in truth, rather than each cabinet minister returning to the House to address the concerns raised by their colleague, a single junior minister – often one with no responsibility at all for the matter at hand – is instead regularly dispatched to read faithfully from a noncommittal script prepared by a civil servant. This can significantly limit the usefulness of the exchange – the stand-in minister will be reluctant to get into a substantive over-and-back conversation about an issue they cannot control. On the flipside, the TD raising the Topical Issue can at least post a video of the exchange online, showcasing themselves as a champion for the constituency, or run to their local radio station or regional newspaper and semi-legitimately accuse the (actual) minister of running from the issue. It matters not that the minister might be abroad for work or genuinely have some other prior commitment.

ß

One time when the minister might at least be assured of actually showing up is during the rostered slot for ministerial questions in the Dáil chamber. Three times a week, for 90 minutes each time, cabinet members present themselves for scrutiny by their fellow deputies, with questions pre-submitted in advance. Each question has two opportunities for follow up, meaning ministers need to be well briefed on any number of live issues within their departments.

These sessions of Ministers' oral questions are the meat and drink of parliamentary business: the primary way for a TD to raise something for their constituents is to put down a question to the minister concerned, usually for written reply, but occasionally with the prospect of being able to pin the minister down for an actual discussion in the chamber.

That means ministers cannot afford to have an off day, and an examination of ministers' diaries confirms they will routinely spend several hours with their special advisors and civil servants ahead of each appearance to make sure all angles are covered.

On at least one occasion, this has resulted in a bit of mischief-making. In 2012, Minister for Health James Reilly was facing a barrage of criticism on all fronts, from the location of new primary care centres to the impact of a recruitment freeze and the ditching of plans to overhaul the health insurance system. Reilly's rostered slot for ministerial questions was fast approaching, and was likely to be an exceptionally difficult session. Any number of opposition TDs would doubtless complain about the impact of staff shortages on their regional hospitals, and with the country still in the era of tough austerity, there were simply no easy answers. That is, unless the questions were unusually sympathetic.

True enough, when the PDF of submitted questions was published on the eve of Reilly's appearance, the list had been swelled by enquiries from coalition backbenchers asking about the progress that had been made cutting waiting lists in their areas. It was the parliamentary equivalent of ballot-stuffing: Fine Gael TDs had diluted the usual batch of critical and hostile questions by flooding the system with more hospitable enquiries. The Minister thus ought to have had an easy ride: instead of being under the cosh for the entire session, he could spend well over an hour discussing how excellent his government was, and illustrating how the waiting times for appointments had been reduced in those select areas. Critical voices would barely get a look-in.

The plan would have worked to perfection, were it not so transparent. Reporters tuning in for the latest round of Question Time immediately smelled a rat because the tone of questions was so imbalanced: it had never been the case before that government backbenchers would line up to throw softballs at the minister, so why were they doing it now? A quick comparison with the questions submitted for Reilly's previous sessions revealed how much of an outlier this one was, and the story was faithfully reported. Press officers quietly bitched about the articles, but could not dispute their substance.

Few ever tried the same routine again.

A third option for active contribution in the Dáil is through the slots of 'private members' business'. The name of this item is slightly misleading: it does not mean, as some outsiders believe, that debates are conducted in private. 'Private' merely means that the business being considered originates from an opposition party, or from a government backbencher. 'Public' business is that which is tabled by the government, the holders of public office. Anything else is 'private' by default.

There are two slots of private members' time in the chamber each week, each two hours in length, rotated among opposition parties in proportion to their size. From 2020 onwards, for example, Sinn Féin has accounted for almost precisely half of all opposition TDs, thus qualifying for one slot per week, on Tuesday evenings. The remainder of the opposition, being organised into smaller groups of roughly equal size, are rostered to a rotating slot every Wednesday morning. A key consideration for each party is to think tactically, and symbolically, about how best to use their rare opportunities to control a window of the Dáil agenda. An acid test of an opposition TD's influence is whether they are able to hold sway within their own party and convince their colleagues to prioritise their specific area of concern; this in turn will grant them a high-profile speaking slot on the topic.

There are a few options available for how this Dáil time might be deployed by opposition groups. They may trigger a debate on legislation of their own, or move non-binding but symbolic motions trying to put pressure on the government to act in certain ways. The potency of the latter has been dramatically diluted in recent years. In the era of traditional majority governments, defeat on a private members' motion was unthinkable: the government would merely exercise the whip to ensure absolute loyalty on the subject and enforce its own position as that of the Dáil as a whole. Defeats were so rare that after being defeated in one such motion in 1987, over a proposed increase in the pupil–teacher ratio, education minister Mary O'Rourke went home believing the government was on the precipice of full collapse. The instinct was understandable: a cabinet that was unable to confidently steer its position through the Dáil could hardly claim to be 'in power' in any material sense.

The dam on this perception burst between 2016 and 2020, when a coalition of Fine Gael and independents held a minority in the chamber, and survived only through the compliance of Fianna Fáil on financial votes and constitutional business like the appointment of ministers (officially titled 'confidence and supply', 'confidence' meaning constitutional matters, and 'supply' meaning spending). Suddenly, the opposition made up 70 per cent of the chamber. If any private members' motion found favour with Fianna Fáil, it was destined to pass ... and cause literally zero tangible effect. Labour's Brendan Howlin remembers being especially annoyed at the reduction of the Dáil to the status of a college debating chamber, considering great matters of state with next to no meaningful authority to direct any change.

In any event, a private members' motion at least forces the government to adopt a stance of its own. A motion on hospital recruitment, for example, might result in the government tabling a countermotion that spells out more specifically its view on a particular aspect. It also allows a visible platform in the chamber for parties to dominate the discussion (while every party has an opportunity to contribute in a debate, the party that 'owns' the slot receives the lion's share of speaking time).

In the most extreme examples, a private members' motion can even result in a binding vote about the future of the government itself. This is the dreaded 'motion of no confidence', where an opposition party invites the Dáil as a whole to declare whether a specific person should remain in the government or not. This vote is not merely symbolic, and has constitutional significance: because government ministers are appointed by (and answerable to) the Dáil as a whole, the loss of confidence is tantamount to a minister being sacked. It is the nuclear option in cases of the gravest controversy, and by definition cannot be used frequently: the rules of the chamber are that the same minister cannot face two motions of no confidence within six months.

In practice, these motions rarely work. The government rallies its troops and uses its majority status to carry the day in any case. Moreover, because a no-confidence motion is the final arrow in the quiver of any opposition party, its defeat will often put a cap on a controversy. A minister in the midst of a scandal who receives a reassuring vote of confidence from the Dáil effectively becomes bulletproof. Leo Varadkar's vote of endorsement after the controversy over his handling of a draft state contract for GPs – personally posted by Varadkar to a personal friend who led a splinter GP body – helped to pour political concrete over the story, even if gardaí were investigating the act for years afterwards.

Nonetheless it is a weapon that sometimes draws fatal injuries. If there is even a sniff of a confidence motion possibly passing, the taoiseach has two choices available. If the scandal is unusually centred around a single minister, and if there is a possibility of the Dáil being happy to approve a replacement, the taoiseach's job is simply to convince the under-fire minister to extinguish the fire by quitting. If this is not an option – because the problem is often a policy itself and not merely the person implementing it – the only course of action is for the government to cut their losses and go to the country. The loss of support from some outside independents was enough to effectively collapse the government in January 2020, when an escalating winter hospital crisis prompted a motion of no confidence in Simon Harris, then the minister for health. Rather than put the question to the Dáil and face a bruising defeat, Leo Varadkar simply called a general election instead. It did not go unremarked around Leinster House that Harris himself had become taoiseach by the time the next election rolled around.

There is limited scope for private members' slots to be availed of by government TDs themselves. Every Thursday evening – at the tail end of the Thursday 'zombie session', and usually long after rural TDs have hit the road for home – there is a final item of business before the House adjourns for the weekend. It alternates every week between discussion on a report filed by an Oireachtas committee – on anything from the state's approach to autism to energy poverty to the funding of sports clubs – and a private members' bill published by individual TDs.

If the sponsor of such a bill can convince the media to pay close enough attention (which isn't a given, as many correspondents will have effectively 'tuned out' by that point of the week), this can be an excellent way to accrue attention and become seen as an influential voice on a specific topic. Moreover, it allows a deputy to advance specific pet projects that might not always be of such national prominence that their party, or their independent grouping, would use its own slot to advance them.

Peadar Tóibín of Aontú used one such slot to try and prohibit the sale of beef products below cost price, garnering favour among small meat producers who felt their own margins being squeezed by supermarkets (who were knowingly selling products at a loss in the hope of attracting more customers through the door). The early calling of the 2024 election denied Eoin Ó Broin of Sinn Féin a chance to promote a bill that would have scrapped the need for planning permission to paint murals on the sides of buildings ('Public art and public art murals make good cities great cities,' he argues).

One ingenious use of a private members' slot, from independent TD Tommy Broughan, was to table legislation on daylight savings time. His Brighter Evenings Bill aimed to provide precisely what the title stated by aligning Ireland with Central European Time so that nightfall might be deferred all year around. As he saw it, brighter evenings – even with the consequence of darker mornings – would result in fewer road accidents, improved energy efficiency and better general wellbeing. 'Members of the human race are children of the light,' he told the Dáil, channelling the TV physics professor Brian Cox.

The bill was unsuccessful; at the time, control of the time zones was still an EU power and the Irish government had no discretion to depart from the European norm. Even if it did have such authority, ministers took a dim view of any initiative which might result in two different time zones on the island, meaning it could be 7 a.m. in Newry but 8 a.m. in Dundalk just down the road. 'If the aim of the Brighter Evenings Bill is to have an extra hour of daylight in the evening, rather than the mornings,' sniffed then Minister for Justice Alan Shatter, 'this could be achieved without legislation by people getting up, going to work and finishing work an hour earlier.'

Nonetheless, as a simple item of publicity-driving, it was fabulously successful. Twice a year, when radio researchers were trying to put together items about the clocks going forward or back, there would forever be one TD they would invite to come on.

🔑

An alternative source of coverage, for a novice deputy with their wits about them, is to get posted to some of the more high-profile Oireachtas committees. At the top of the tree is the Public Accounts Committee (PAC), which has the right to scrutinise the accounts of government departments and state agencies, and to haul their top brass in for grilling.

Government ministers and major opposition party leaders are not everyday members of committees – ministers attend only when their own performances or proposals are being scrutinised – so the everyday grunt work is done by government backbenchers and members of the opposition parties. Though nobody can ever predict what news will fall from the heavens – like in the summer of 2023, when a payments controversy at RTÉ thrust the Oireachtas Media Committee into the public spotlight – the PAC has a standing role in parliamentary theatre. It is no coincidence that the likes of Simon Harris, Mary Lou McDonald, Paschal Donohoe, Eoghan Murphy and Shane Ross all became so prominent in the early 2010s: when public spending was being ruthlessly slashed, media-savvy TDs could exploit the platform of the PAC to build up healthy profiles of their own.

One consequence of committee membership is early access to major or significant announcements. Witnesses before an Oireachtas committee will routinely send copies of their opening statements a day or two in advance, which are then distributed to committee members alongside any supporting documents. This is to give those committee members a chance to prepare their lines of inquiry for the meeting to come. However, journalists looking for a decent yarn will often contact committee members asking for copies of the statements (which will enter the public domain anyway as soon as the meeting begins), and the more enterprising deputies eventually realise they can curry some favour by passing such notes along proactively. The politician who shares the most newsworthy nugget might also be the one who gets asked to provide a reaction for that evening's news bulletins, or the following morning's newspaper. Sometimes, in cases where a politician is on a committee for which they have no real interest, they might even ask journalists to suggest lines of enquiry.

Some politicians – especially those from outside Dublin, who have nothing else to do on a weeknight, or those Dubliners without young families – might agree to take up invitations onto panel shows, like RTÉ's *Prime Time*, *The Tonight Show* on Virgin Media, or *The Late Debate* on RTÉ Radio One. Such postings can often be suicide missions: at times of crisis or controversy, the politician will inevitably find themselves defending a losing position. It's short-term pain for long-term gain: someone who is seen to serve their party by taking regular punishment beatings on air might eventually be rewarded with a better job of their own.

Some infamous examples prove this. In 2013, for example, the Dáil and Seanad sat overnight passing emergency legislation to liquidate the former Anglo Irish Bank. Rumours had begun to circulate that day about the future of the nationalised bank, amid a complicated scheme to escape an expensive interest repayment, but it was felt that rather than risk a mass withdrawal of cash the following day, the most prudent course of action was to wind up the bank entirely. This required the government to remain silent about the situation until the close of business on one evening, then announce its proposals and pass emergency laws placing the bank into emergency liquidation before the doors opened the next morning. Politicians were put on notice that evening of a possible overnight sitting, and President Michael D. Higgins was summoned home from an official visit to Italy so that he could consider the bill and have it signed into law before the markets had an opportunity to react the next morning.

Such overnight sittings are an occasion when the veneer of calm, orderly organisation within government can peel away. The Dáil was supposed to start debating this bill at 10:30 p.m. but, due to publication delays and the need for members to actually read the thing, didn't start the job until midnight. Fine Gael backbencher Paschal Donohoe was dispatched to Ballymount to be the government representative on TV3's nightly *Tonight with Vincent Browne* panel show. The programme was due to start at 11 p.m., and Donohoe took the assignment on the expectation that he could echo the arguments made by Minister for Finance Michael Noonan in his opening Dáil speech. At the very least, someone in government could have briefed him on what exactly the legislation was intended to achieve, and the mechanics by which a complex financial transaction could be undertaken in the dead of night.

But not only was no such briefing actually forthcoming, the programme producers decided to start the show at 10 p.m., to capitalise on the national appetite for clarity in a moment of confusion – leaving Donohoe to gamely address questions with the blunt tenacity of a cricket nightwatchman, offering non-specific lines parroting the ethos of government support for the financial sector while seeking to limit the burden on taxpayers.

Finally reprieved as the show went off air at 1 a.m. – having stayed on late to carry the opening of the Dáil debate live – Donohoe returned to Leinster House and asked why government officials had left him high and dry, sent on live TV to act as a salesman for a plan that hadn't been explained to him. Their answer – only partly a joke – was that they had spent the evening watching Donohoe on telly, hoping that he himself could work out a concise explanation of the byzantine scheme which could then be repeated by the department.

TV3 allowed Donohoe to keep a *Tonight with Vincent Browne*-branded mug as a souvenir of his chaotic night; for years it retained pride of place in his ministerial offices. It was little coincidence that when the plum junior ministry for EU affairs became vacant only five months later, Donohoe was the man rewarded; by 2016 Donohoe had become minister for public expenditure, working alongside the same Michael Noonan in the drafting of national budgets and shaping the country's fiscal future.

♟

Many who tune in to Leaders' Questions on television are quickly frustrated by a relatively new phenomenon in Irish politics. The head of the lead opposition party might stand up and complain about the main issue of the day, with the government playing defensively and insisting the controversy is not as it appears; another opposition leader then stands up to raise the same issue … but instead of following up from where their predecessor began, they will introduce the subject as if they were the first to do so.

From the outside this is a bizarre and seemingly inexplicable act. Imagine a lid stuck on a jar, where someone is only eventually able to remove it thanks to the efforts of someone else who loosened it first. Why would the second person introduce the topic afresh, and ask questions that ignored the detail already revealed to the predecessor?

The reason is a performative one: it is now very important not just to ask a question, but in an era of social media and rapid sharing of videos, to be *seen* to do it. If you speak in the chamber, but don't post a video of it on X or Instagram or Facebook afterwards, did it really happen? And in that case, why would you post a video that doesn't start out by explaining the problem you're facing?

This dynamic is a single insightful illustration of how performative politics has come, and how savvy press officers will try to gain maximal exposure for their masters. Where once the only goal of a Dáil exchange was to get a politician to answer a question, perhaps by exploiting the weaknesses exposed in a previous answer, now it's equally about being seen to ask the question in the first place. Indeed, the author has seen some instances where an opposition TD has posted a video of themselves challenging a minister on some doubtless critical topic, but omitted the minister's level-headed answer, preferring to present themselves as a tireless crusader rather than present the rather boring fruits of their labour.

This is seen as a double-edged sword by politicians themselves: if social media is now a beast with which they must contend, there is recognition that politicians helped to create the monster. 'When we started putting videos on Facebook,' says one, 'the idea was to give a wider platform to the stuff we were saying, which people might not have seen on TV or anywhere else. Now, you have people applying the same principle, but they're not coming at it with the inside knowledge that we did – they're standing on the outside, not realising the greater nuance of things, and using the same techniques against us.'

There is also a perception that the desire to ask questions for an online audience, rather than for immediate parliamentary scrutiny, makes life easier for the government. 'You can see it in Simon Harris, that he loves the joust,' says one of the former taoiseach's contemporaries. 'And you can see, if he gets a question from Mary Lou McDonald and then gets the same question two or three times later, he's just having the time of his life.'

Others simply regret how performative politics has now become, and how maximising exposure online simultaneously means having to make a less substantial version of your case. Some speak of the challenge of making a Dáil speech that makes a substantive contribution to the debate while also yielding a shorter and snappier point that can be presented online.

'We're being told that people are consuming their news on TikTok now, or Instagram or whatever – so you have to, when you're doing your work, make sure there's an element of it that's presentable in that format,' says Labour's Duncan Smith. 'That means you are then thinking, "Well, I need to make this speech, but I also need to get this point across, that I can get into thirty seconds and go up in a clip …" I find myself constantly trying to check against that.'

If they want to play that game, smaller parties will look enviously at the ability of larger ones to stage-manage their contributions. 'You'll see a [Sinn Féin] spokesperson speaking for eight minutes, then a deputy spokesperson speaking for four, and then other TDs getting to speak for a minute each – and all of their speeches will have been written for them, and almost designed for social media consumption. It's very disciplined and very well organised, because it means the spokesperson can give a substantive speech, and their colleagues can speak almost solely so they can tell the local papers about it, and also for the purposes of getting a video for Instagram.'

Social media is a live-by-the-sword, die-by-the-sword environment. A few younger TDs have grown up without ever knowing a world without it; some older ones are so well established in their constituencies that they can afford to bypass it entirely. Those in the middle will often find the waters are choppy. Gary Gannon's arrival onto the political scene, as a then-independent councillor in 2014, coincided with the zenith of Facebook as a campaign platform (by his own admission, he has been somewhat bypassed by the rise of TikTok as the modern-day platform of choice). As a millennial TD he is the same age as many of the most ardent always-on internet users. Still, there can be onslaughts: in 2022 Gannon was the only local representative who vocally defended the use of a former industrial plant in East Wall to house asylum-seekers; the proposal had gained national attention from right-wing nationalists and the pushback was often toxic. 'The level of abuse then was fairly vitriolic,' he says, before recognising that he probably would never have entered politics if social media was not a weapon in his armoury. 'I suppose you have to take the rough with the smooth. I've developed a fairly hard skin.'

Often there can be no substitute for the old-fashioned grafting of knocking on doors and picking up phones. Fine Gael's Noel Rock found the job demanded two permanent parallel goals, communication and achievement. 'Aptly for my name, you're a permanent Sisyphus,' says Rock, recalling the Greek myth of the ruler condemned to spend eternity pushing a boulder up a hill. 'You're pushing rocks up hills, and telling people exactly what point on the hill each rock is at, what you're trying to achieve and when you'll achieve it.

'Ultimately, communication alone won't do it if you're getting nowhere – that veers into "busy fool" territory. But you need something to communicate, and that means you do have to "achieve" repeatedly. That's especially important if you're on the government's side of the House.'

A particular highlight for him was stopping a plan to shut the Finglas East post office on Glasnevin Avenue. The outgoing postmistress had left and An Post, in cost-cutting mode, wanted to shutter the facility entirely instead of recruiting a replacement. Rock knew the battle to save it would be tough – almost Sisyphean – but had to at least try. 'Someone I've known for years, who worked in An Post, initially said I hadn't a hope – but we got a campaign going and, crucially, got some incredibly supportive data for our case.' Four thousand people signed a petition he organised seeking to illustrate the demand for continued services.

'After some months An Post relented. The person from An Post still cites it to this day as the biggest political surprise he has ever seen, and I love that.'

11

DID YOU GET THE CALL?

Between Leinster House and Government Buildings is an over-head glass tunnel with a footbridge. It is used often, but only by a small coterie of people. At one end is the Oireachtas complex and the seat of parliament; at the other are two corridors of ministerial offices, out of which ministers and their advisors can work while the Dáil and Seanad are sitting.

The bridge is often heavily watched. On specific days, journalists will loiter nearby, or at the smoking area underneath, their eyes trained on the comings and goings. Press photographers will camp outside the closest gate, a good thirty yards away, their tele-photo lenses fixed on the bridge. Both groups moan in displeasure when the Leinster House ushers, wise to the bridge's sudden pop-ularity, draw the Venetian blinds to offer privacy to those inside.

Most politicians never have cause to use this bridge. The first time they do is one of the biggest days of their lives.

They have got The Call. Their leader wants to see them.

Those walking that bridge are being invited over to meet the taoiseach and be appointed as a member of the Government of Ireland.

♟

Despite what might be presumed on the outside, many prospec-tive ministers simply don't know if they're on the list to get The Call. Heather Humphreys was in the members' bar having a cup of tea on reshuffle day in 2014, three years into her maiden term as a TD, one of 76 Fine Gael TDs, 19 of whom would hold ministries of some sort. Colleagues were speculating about possible nominees, but Humphreys was finding the parlour game tiring so returned to her office to break the back of some more constituency work. 'I was phoning some school about something-or-other, and I got a call on the mobile – because I was on the landline – from Sarah, Enda Kenny's personal secretary, to see would I go over and see him.' Even then, naïvely, she thought it would be a pep talk from the taoiseach encouraging her to keep working and that a ministerial job might come her way later. Instead, she was to be nominated as minister for arts and heritage. 'Opportunities come to pass, not to pause,' her husband counselled her.

Even those in the closest orbit to the leader of a coalition party can't be sure they'll get a job: outsiders might presume Richard Bruton had advance notice of his cabinet appointment in 1994, when his brother John was the taoiseach of the 'Rainbow Coalition', of Fine Gael, Labour and Democratic Left. But even the taoiseach's brother needed to wait for The Call to find out he would be one of his brother's seven Fine Gael cabinet nominees.

'The run-up to it is feeling like a little boy, going into the principal's office and wondering what's going to befall you,' says Bruton. 'It's an unusual atmosphere. A lot of people are sitting in their offices wondering will they get The Call, and people walking up and walking back [outside the corridor] – and trying to judge from their smiles, or their grim faces, what has befallen them. It is a very strange process – particularly if you're going into government, and you move from a very collegiate sort of front bench, to suddenly, some are being selected, and some are falling by the wayside. It's quite a frosty period.'

Deciding who and who not to call is a new taoiseach's biggest challenge. Leo Varadkar remarks wryly that the best cabinet is one where you can give 15 jobs to 22 people.

'It's not a meritocracy,' admits one serial appointee. 'You don't always get selected because you're the best: there's geography and gender and all sorts of things.' Geography can be a thorny quali-fication: Cork always expects a cabinet seat, to the consternation of Kerry, which then expects one too. Connacht perennially feels under-represented, as do the north-west and the border region. In forming coalitions, while each party generally leaves the others to their own devices and to nominate whomsoever they choose, there also needs to be consideration of the broader geographical and demographic composition. Leo Varadkar tried to draft his cabinet lineup by writing the name of each Fine Gael TD on an ice cream stick, with symbols to denote their gender and length of service, and then laying them atop a map of the country.

That was a luxury afforded to Varadkar by the nature of the 2016–20 cabinet, a minority government in which Fine Gael held almost every ministerial role, save for a few independents. By 2020 the situation was remarkably different, and Fine Gael had only six senior ministries, as their new cabinet colleagues Fianna Fáil and the Greens took six and three respectively. Ministerial nominations were made in three silos – no party wanting to be seen to meddle in the affairs of others – which led to a geograph-ically skewed cabinet. Cork South-Central alone had three min-isters, including Micheál Martin as taoiseach; Dublin West had two, in Leo Varadkar and Roderic O'Gorman; Wicklow had two from Greystones alone, in Simon Harris and Stephen Donnelly, but the west coast had no full minister from Malin Head down to Kerry and had to make do with two 'super junior' reps. The tripartite composition of the top 15 then had to be remedied with the appointment of junior ministers.

It is also the case that leaders sometimes prefer to leave talent outside the ministerial ranks, partly as a rebuke, partly to demon-strate boldness in appointments, and partly because they'll be so busy in government that they'll need to keep eyes and ears within the party. This author has some firsthand familiarity of presumptive ministers having their fingers burned, and having to cancel pre-arranged media appearances when The Call did not come their way.

And, remarkably, there are cases where the equilibrium collapses at the last minute – because someone refuses a ministerial appointment, or doesn't want the specific job they are being given. This is known to have happened once or twice; one case was that of Mary Mitchell O'Connor, who was demoted from the senior to junior ranks in 2017 and who refused one proposed appointment before accepting an alternative offer of becoming a junior minister for higher education. Those involved were grateful that the refusal came towards the end of the process, where the knock-on consequences and resultant on-the-fly reshuffling were limited.

☗

If The Call does come, it's quick, and amounts to little more than a summoning from a private secretary: 'The Taoiseach would like to see you in his office immediately, please.' The TD promptly scuttles from wherever they were, and makes their way to the tunnel and across into Government Buildings, where they are escorted to the taoiseach's office on the opposite side of the building.

There, the mood is cordial but businesslike: the taoiseach is usually only a few hours in the job, and has 16 or 17 of these meetings to conduct in a very short window.

I'm sure you're wondering why I've asked you here, as a polite and rhetorical icebreaker.

I'm appointing you the minister for whatever, the taoiseach might say, *with a particular focus on X, Y and Z.*

There is barely time for a 'Wonderful, I'm delighted, what a privilege, thank you, Taoiseach', and subsequent pleasantries. After roughly 90 seconds the newly minted minister is sent on their way and led back to the bridge, ready to go either back to Leinster House and their parliamentary offices, or to the ministerial corridor within Government Buildings and the office that will now be designated as theirs. They will be intercepted by a coterie of civil servants and other operatives, offering quick briefings on the schedule for the rest of the day and what might be expected of them.

The phone will start ringing. The secretary general of the new department, the highest-ranking civil servant in the new minister's organisation, will be calling with a congratulatory message and a formal introduction. The private secretary, who coordinates the diary and logistical matters, is dispatched to meet the nominee, arriving with a series of briefing papers, and the schedule of meetings that have been lined up for the next day. The same schedule is passed onto the two gardaí who will serve as the minister's drivers.

The nominee will only have a few hours of liberty at most, and is expected to keep news of their promotion to a tightly controlled inner circle: in principle their new appointment is supposed to be announced to the Dáil by the taoiseach. An unprepared minister who didn't already have their hair newly trimmed, or come to work wearing a fresh suit, might have time to fetch some new threads, but is unlikely to get out in person for fear of meeting too many inquisitors asking about their new appointment.

Nonetheless the news gets out. Often the first person told about an incumbent minister's appointment – even before their spouse – is their special advisor, many of whom are hired specifically to act as media liaisons. Some will find the information too juicy to keep to themselves, and will eventually reply to some of the dozens of inquisitive messages bombarding their phones. One of those journalists will then post the news online, and the appointment is effectively national canon before the taoiseach is able to line up the new cabinet for a ceremonial photo and lead them into the Dáil for their official presentation. Even this process is subject to some ceremonial rigour: ministers are lined up, and led into the chamber, in order of seniority. After the taoiseach comes the tánaiste, then the leaders of any other coalition parties, then the minister for finance (as the only other cabinet role which gets an explicit mention in the constitution). Others are then lined up in order of length of service. It is also practice for the names of the ministers, as formally announced to the chamber for approval, to be listed in this order.

Those with good news will have had enough time by now to pass it to their families, who might make it to Kildare Street in time to sit in the public gallery as their loved ones are announced to the world as new members of the government. There will be little or no time to pop up and say hello, however: the nominees are expected to sit in the chamber while the Dáil goes through the motions of debating, and eventually approving, their appointments as ministers. Once that's done, it's off to Áras an Uachtaráin – previously in a fleet of swanky black luxury cars, more recently in an executive minibus – where the appointment is made official by the president.

The seals of office are presented one by one. The taoiseach is handed two, one as head of the government and one as a member thereof. The others get one seal each, polished silver bearing a harp and the words '*Éire – an Rialtas*' (Ireland – the Government). Those who are curious enough to read the underside of the seal will find that it bears no link to their actual department: the names and configurations of government departments are relatively fluid, and can change overnight, but the seals remain unchanged. Eamon Gilmore, on becoming minister for foreign affairs, plucked up his seal to find the words '*Aire Cosanta*' – Minister for Defence. Many others don't have a chance to inspect their seals: once the photographs are finished, the seals are collected up and restored to a safe at the Áras, often before their temporary custodians have had a chance to look at them at all.

Assuming there's a new taoiseach being appointed on the same day, tradition dictates they hold their inaugural ceremonial meeting in the State Dining Room of the Áras, but there will be little of substance on the agenda: the new taoiseach might merely lay out a potted version of their political agenda, invite other ministers to do the same, and adjourn for the night. The table around which they sit has experience of more substantial business: the one currently in the State Dining Room previously resided in Leinster House. Prior to the full development of the adjoining Government Buildings as a separate home for the executive branch, it literally served as the cabinet table. Every government in the history of an independent Ireland has, at some time, sat around it.

The organising of cabinet appointments, even in the times when Fianna Fáil would have sufficient TDs to govern alone, has always been relatively scattergun. The late Albert Reynolds only realised that he had been given a full cabinet job in 1979 when political correspondents told him they could figure out 14 of the appointments but couldn't quite ascertain who had got the fifteenth. In issuing The Call, Taoiseach Charlie Haughey had merely told Reynolds he would be given the job of sorting out 'the fucking telephone system', and Reynolds – Haughey's eventual successor – presumed he was becoming a minister of state at what was then the Department of Posts and Telegraphs. He hadn't realised he was becoming the full cabinet minister in that department.

♟

The pomp of a full appointment is in stark contrast to the relatively muted, and in some cases entirely underwhelming, handling of 'ministers of state', more commonly labelled as junior ministers. While junior ministries are technically filled by the cabinet acting as a whole, in practice the party leader has the only say and the names are presented to the rest of cabinet as a *fait accompli* in the days after the senior positions are doled out. Compared to the national news attention paid to the formation of a government, assignment of the junior positions often commands relatively little interest beyond the political bubble and the immediate families of those involved. In some ways this gives party leaders a tougher job: an appointment that appears counterintuitive or unnatural inside Leinster House may be well received by outsiders or industry, but overlooking the wrong candidates for junior ministries can create many enemies within the gates. Do under-served regions get their fair share of jobs? Do the appointments demonstrate to newer backbenchers that their youth will not hold them back? Are the junior ministers a compatible fit, personality-wise, with the senior ones in the same department? And, in a coalition, is there a balance where no party gets a stranglehold on jobs within a single department? (When the Greens' leader Eamon Ryan took the job of minister for transport, Fine Gael insisted on taking a junior ministry for roads and air transport, for fear that an environmentalist would abandon roads projects in rural areas. 'We needed someone in there to supervise him,' concluded one party source.)

In the older era of single-party government, new ministers were convened on the night before their formal unveiling, so that all would find out *en masse* the jobs to which they were being assigned. Whether by accident or design, this allowed for some jobs to be redesigned on the hoof: there is at least one documented case of two TDs feeling underprepared for the junior ministries they were about to be given, and simply swapping jobs in a mutual act of self-accommodation.

Trying to get the correct balance of geography, gender and party can sometimes mean the choreography of getting The Call for a junior ministry is far less polished than that of a full cabinet job. A common thread is that The Call, when it comes, is much later than people expect. Unlike full ministries, which can dominate a new taoiseach's thinking for the days before appointment, junior ministries are often a less meditative and more scattergun process. Junior transport minister James Lawless had arrived in Leinster House on the Thursday morning of his eventual appointment, hoping he might be at the top of Micheál Martin's shortlist for a vacant junior ministry, even showing up unexpectedly at Leaders' Questions to sit behind the tánaiste in an act of visual-solidarity-cum-buttering-up. But no phone call came, so Lawless hopped on the train back to Kildare … and got The Call just as his wife picked him up from the station, necessitating a quick spin back to Dublin.

Brendan Griffin had also been hoping for The Call far earlier than it came, during Leo Varadkar's takeover in June 2017. The appointments were due to be announced on a Tuesday; on the Monday evening the 35-year-old brought his dog for a late walk as dusk fell in the week of the summer solstice, hoping for the phone to ring as he walked. Having been left disappointed with appointments in 2016, Griffin was hopeful of promotion – and then, when The Call never came, calm in acceptance. 'I remember the auld dog put her muzzle into my lap, and I was rubbing her head, and I thought, "Fuck it, 'twill be grand, 'twill be fine," I started feeling very philosophical about the whole thing.'

His wife had lit a candle in the gable window of the home, and coming home at nightfall, 'there was a great sense of peace, and just a feeling of calm. I put the dog into the shed, and I slept like a baby. Absolutely like a baby – just turned off the light, gone … so much so that I didn't hear the phone ringing at stupid o'clock, six fifty-five or whatever, until it was almost gone.'

Griffin had left his phone in the walk-in wardrobe adjoining the bedroom, and roused just too late to pick up the call. 'A missed call from Leo Varadkar. *Fuck it.* The next thing, the text message – "You have one new voice message" – comes through. And I'm thinking, this is going to be one now where he says, "I'm very sorry I wasn't able to appoint you to a position, but I want you to be the chairman of whatever." And so, I actually took the phone up to the kitchen, because I didn't want my wife to see what my reaction would be – and I thought it was going to be disappointing, especially if it was a voice message, because you'd want to deliver the good news in person.

'So I went up to the kitchen and dialled it, and listened to the voicemail, and, "Hi, Brendan, it's Leo here" – as if I didn't know who it was! – "Sorry I missed you there. No need to call back. There's a position that's come up in the Department of Transport, Tourism and Sport, so I'd like you to be my Minister of State for Tourism and Sport, if you'll take it. I'll see you in Dublin later on." I went down and played it for my wife, and the rest of the day is a blur.'

How someone accepts an appointment as a junior minister can reveal much about their personal ambition. If they're appointed on the same day as a full cabinet, a junior ministry – even if the holder is becoming a 'super junior' with the right to attend cabinet meetings – can seem like a consolation prize for the bruised ego of a TD who hoped for a 'real' cabinet job. Others with fewer personal expectations will gladly receive the appointment under any circumstances, content to take the title of 'Minister' as the ceiling of their own career aspirations. Still others might hungrily take the appointment and get to work immediately, hoping to prove their capacity in the job and to be first in line to fill a vacancy in cabinet proper.

If the latter is the case, and the new job is a stepping stone to bigger things, the mission objective is to run a steady ship. 'My overriding feeling when I was appointed', one former junior minister says, 'was not to let the senior minister down. In the majority of cases I was in a room, or at a meeting, or taking Dáil questions as proxy for them – my sole concern was making sure I didn't fuck things up for them.'

12

THE WALNUT TABLE

Much like the choice of Leinster House itself, the meeting quarters for the cabinet emerged more by accident than design. Under the partition of Ireland imposed by Britain in 1920, a 'Parliament of Southern Ireland' was due to act as the main legislature for the 26 counties. A busted flush from its very conception, the parliament was only recognised by four southern unionist members, and is thought only to have met once before adjourning indefinitely. The unionist MPs chose, as their meeting venue, the council room in the Royal College of Science on Dublin's well-to-do Merrion Street, just across the road from the historic birthplace of Arthur Wellesley, the first Duke of Wellington, a British war hero and two-time prime minister.

By accident of history, the new Oireachtas made its own headquarters next door, borrowing and eventually buying Leinster House from the Royal Dublin Society, with sittings taking place in the RDS's former lecture theatre. The slow expansion of the new Free State government eventually meant occupying the adjoining part of the college nearby as a workspace and, eventually, holding weekly meetings of the cabinet in the same council room that once hosted the abortive lame-duck Southern Parliament. The first government of the Free State took the formal title of Executive Council, and so 'Council Room' now refers both to that prototype government and the governing body of the College of Science that came before it. The Royal College of Science eventually became incorporated into University College Dublin, and fully abandoned its Merrion Street facilities when UCD left its various city-centre buildings for its own 360-acre campus in Belfield.

Today the council room is designed to marry history and modernity. The walls are lined with portraits of former leaders and cabinets containing ornately bound copies of statutes passed by the eighteenth-century Parliament of Ireland. The furniture, commissioned in 2004, is curvaceous and contemporary. The central table is oval shaped, almost like a human eye, with different varieties of walnut wood set into its centre. Each chair is fashioned from 88 separate pieces of walnut, without a single straight line. Each seat is padded with modest leatherette cushioning, intended in principle to offer reasonable comfort without inducing any slouching. (The restrained comfort has not stopped the occasional nap: at least one former minister is suspected of having fallen asleep at the table.)

In those chairs sit the taoiseach, tánaiste and 13 other cabinet-level ministers, plus the attorney general, the secretary general of the Department of the Taoiseach (nominally the 'secretary to the government', as the country's highest-ranking civil servant), and 'super junior' ministers with the right to attend but not to participate in votes. The latter disclaimer is a constitutional sop; in truth the cabinet almost never votes on matters. If someone is so opposed to an idea as to threaten a veto, it is usually parked and left to be thrashed out at a lower level.

'The first time you walk in there,' says one, 'you do feel history weighing on you.'

Ω

Though not every TD sets out in life with the ambition of becoming a minister, there is no getting away from the ambition that many develop once they have landed in Leinster House. 'There are only fifteen important people in the country,' one TD has ruefully declared. 'If you're not in cabinet, you're nobody.'

Those who enter politics genuinely for altruism, or perhaps because they are driven by a single issue, quickly realise that even the best-administered campaigns and the most vociferous soundbites in the chamber have a limited threshold for success. Ultimately, the buck stops with a small coterie of people, gathered around the walnut table in the council room.

It is said that, upon appointment, civil servants will test the mettle of a new minister by immediately stacking their diary with endless introductory meetings and getting-to-know-you sessions. The purpose of this, supposedly, is to see if the minister will meekly accept the diary as laid out for them, or if they will refuse some meetings to set their own agenda. Those who resist the schedule are recognised as having clear political priorities; those who don't are putty in the hands of the 'Permanent Government'.

Few of the ministers who spoke for this book believed this story to be true – at least, not from the perspective of this being an acid test of a minister's political backbone. It is definitely true that the diary is stacked from day one, but with meetings and introductory engagements that are sincerely aimed at helping a minister to learn the ropes of their role. The potential danger for a minister is the accidental portrayal of someone who is willing to be steered rather than to do the steering themselves.

'You'll go in, and what they will do is, they will try and bury you with briefings and everything,' says one. 'Your response should be to bury them back with questions.'

Even at that, those who want to feel they understand the role – which is a prerequisite for someone appointed at the beginning of a government's term, and thus facing the possibility of a few years in the job – feel compelled to accept as many of those appointments as possible. The more people you've met, the principle is, the more relationships you might be able to lean on. This is especially true of junior ministers, who are not always perceived as being authoritative, and whose rapport with officials might be more important in achieving anything of substance during their tenure.

'I was just saying yes to absolutely everything,' says one minister, of this induction period. 'It was exhausting, but I was saying yes to everything. It wasn't until time passed on that I felt I could say, "No, I'm not going to take that meeting," or, "No, we're not doing that," or, "That doesn't need to be two hours, we can do that in thirty minutes."'

Politicians, eventually, do need to eat as well. 'I don't want a fucking lunch meeting,' quips another TD. 'I won't get to eat lunch.'

Diary pressures aside, all new ministers are acutely aware of the need to strike the balance by pursuing their own plans while keeping the civil servants onside in doing so. Criminally undervalued or unacceptably pampered, depending on your view, there is no getting away from their importance and influence – and the value of having collaborative relationships with the ones in your orbit.

'Most civil servants' definition of a good minister is one who can recite their briefing notes, and get the resources they need,' one incumbent says. Even those with a command of the brief, and intent on making real change in a new portfolio, are sometimes advised not to rock the boat in the early days so as to create a favourable impression with the staff working underneath them. 'It's a bit like the Vikings: they ended up running the place by becoming more Irish than the Irish themselves. You have a better chance of getting them to move in your favour later if you act like you're going undercover and pretending to be one of them.'

One former secretary general, approached for interview for this book, claimed not to recognise the portrayal of civil servants as an occasional impediment to political action. 'Our job is to serve the people,' they said, 'and the people choose their leaders who make the decisions on their behalf.'

Really? Don't civil servants ever push back against a political idea? 'Well, I didn't say that …

'If you imagine a department as being like a business – which it's not, but let's imagine it is – then the sec-gen is the CEO, and the minister is the chairman who's pulling the strings at the top. It's not reasonable for a minister to be able to run a department they've never been in before – that's my job.'

The analogy is an interesting one. Some businesses are dominated by their CEOs, with the chairs exercising only a supervisory role; others have more activist chairs, while the CEOs feel directly accountable and need to display their worth. Perhaps the same is true of ministers and their departments: each department has its own subculture, and some are more easily bent to the will of a minister than others.

ʒ

Those with more experience of ministerial office – or at the very least, those who have been paying very close attention to the work of others – find there are some ways to steer the directions of the department without necessarily coming across as too confrontational.

One is the little-understood requirement to produce a 'Statement of Strategy'. By law each department is required to produce a three-year statement of its overall goals within six months of the appointment of a new senior minister. These are regularly overlooked by politicians and press, treated as if they are mere corporate obligations, banal and politically meaningless. In practice, however, these are more pivotal documents for civil servants, laying out the overarching bureaucratic goals for the forthcoming three years – in the most optimistic cases, outlining a desired end goal, and then proposing some stepping stones to measure progress along the way. Politicians generally tend to think the

Programme for Government is the most important guiding document to their work; civil servants charged with navigating the path are more bound by the terms of their employer's strategy statement instead.

This means that within a few months of entering a department, a minister will either seize an important opportunity to put their foot down and determine the everyday priorities of the staff underneath them … or allow themselves to be overruled, and find that the bureaucracy of the civil service has swallowed them up instead. Ministers report different experiences in terms of how forthcoming their own civil servants were about the significance of this process; some found the document was barely mentioned to them, and then presented afterwards almost as a *fait accompli*. Others – including the few whose appointments entailed the creation of brand-new departments – found the bureaucrats much more forthcoming in asking for political guidance on the task to come.

As a general rule, civil servants will already have taken a broad stab at interpreting the Programme for Government and trying to figure out plans for its implementation. When a new minister arrives in their office for the first time, therefore, they are not facing a blank desk and a blank sheet of paper: officials will already have charted a basic path. But civil servants also know that a minister who takes little interest in the Statement of Strategy can eventually be bent to the will of the officials. Some departments will produce statements that effectively amount to a single flow chart; those are the ones in which high-ranking civil servants are seen as particularly powerful. More bulky strategic documents likely reflect that the minister concerned has been particularly active in drafting.

'It is amazing how few people end up running departments with the understanding, in advance, that politicians have one priority, and civil servants have another,' says one governmental veteran. 'The civil servants don't work for the minister, they work for the department. The Statement of Strategy is the opportunity to merge those two sets of priorities. If the minister misses the boat and doesn't use the opportunity to commit the staff to the same goals, they might as well not be there.

'Civil servants get a bad rap, but they are ultimately motivated by what they see as the national interest: the best strategic outcomes for the country, the most workable fix, the cheapest option. In fact, pursuing the cheapest option is probably why they get such a bad rap, because often from the outside that just looks like stinginess. So if you don't manage to merge your priorities with theirs, the department will definitely keep ticking over – but your own priorities won't feature.'

One other reason why the Statement of Strategy is important is that the government's own agenda may have been defined haphazardly. Some political parties are very assiduous about having their election manifestos drafted by the frontbench spokespersons, who have spent the previous years developing particular expertise in their specific portfolios. Others can be a little more casual: depending on a spokesperson's relationship with the party leader, manifesto chapters can be submitted and immediately discarded, replaced by something more centrally concocted. Marc MacSharry insists he drafted a fully costed tourism manifesto for Fianna Fáil's 2020 election campaign, which never saw the light of day. MacSharry, whose headstrong and pugnacious tendencies often saw him out of favour with the party centrally, reckons Micheál Martin's small inner core of advisors wrote much of the manifesto themselves.

As a result a party can, sometimes, go into a general election proposing a suite of policies that have not been drafted by anyone with in-depth knowledge of that portfolio. Moreover, because only a small subset of each party's front bench is invited to form a negotiating team, pledges in any specific area might have to be dropped as makeweights in the give and take of inter-party bar-ter. The end result is that a document put forward for agreement by party members, and intended to be a political roadmap for the country for the next five years, can feel very hastily patched together. A collegial front bench can prove useful on this front: if a frontbencher is personally friendly with any of the negotiators, they can impress upon them the need for certain points to be reflected in the final deal. Often the final concessions that seal a deal concern issues for which nobody was prepared to stand up.

'There are usually one or two policy wonks in the room along-side the negotiators, so there is genuine reason to have confidence in a programme for government when it is finally produced,' says one person with firsthand experience of these inter-party talks. 'But in absolute truth, these deals can be a bit of a hodgepodge of confu-sion – you have negotiators who don't know an area, trying to stand up for a party manifesto which might also not have been written by someone who knows that area.' This former negotiator stops, almost in horror. 'It's actually a bit mortifying if you think about it.'

'If you can get something written into the Programme for Government,' says one beneficiary of a well-connected negotiat-ing team, 'you'll have your foot well inside the door.'

𝕽

Two unexpected difficulties faced by new appointments relate to the human resources aspect of managing the extra staff that come with the job. As a mere TD, a politician has two staff and is able to run a fairly simple ship. Even the lowest-ranking junior ministers have five staff, including drivers, and may have little or no experi-ence in how to work as a line manager. A senior cabinet minister will have still more staff to contend with.

'Knowing how to task them, manage them, training, perfor-mance management, organisation, running a distributed workplace, hybrid working, office security, motivation, team building … it's all up to you,' says one. 'And unless you've run a small business previously, we have no preparation or knowledge of how to do this. HR in a small business is such a challenge that the likes of ISME run helplines and support workshops, but we're totally on our own.'

Some also confess to being surprised at how small this personal team is: aside from their two garda drivers working in rotation, a minister in a senior cabinet job will only have two special advisors on top of their existing staff, who remain on parliamentary duties. The only other addition is a ministerial private secretary whose functions are largely around diary management. 'The bit you don't appreciate [before joining] is that the team around the minister is very small,' says one former advisor. 'It's the minister, a private secretary, and two advisors. You have the wider departmental apparatus but when it comes to the crunch, or if you're in a difficult spot, it's just the core team in the eye of the storm. The minister and the advisors end up bonding very tightly simply because of the nature of decision-making.'

Almost inadvertently, because of how tightly these professional bonds develop – in a job that entails lengthy hours and little respite – the running of a country can end up evolving into 15 separate silos, with each minister in the near-permanent company of advisors. If a minister hasn't managed to win over their civil servants, the relatively small team around them is of little help in swimming against the tide.

One real area where this problem crystallises is when it comes to the annual negotiations on the budget. In the weeks before Budget Day, the minister for public expenditure holds a series of bilateral meetings with every other member of the cabinet, where the other minister presents a condensed wish list of priorities for the next year, and the minister for public expenditure generally tuts disapprovingly about how expensive they will all be. Nobody is spared this: even the taoiseach has to go cap in hand, looking for additional money for some of the few projects managed centrally within the Department of the Taoiseach. It would take a ballsy minister to turn down a funding request from a taoiseach, but equally it would take a ballsy taoiseach to look for money that might be more meaningfully spent in another department.

'I learned very quickly that money solves a lot of problems, and if you manage to get good budgets, you are the darling,' says Heather Humphreys. 'If you don't, you're screwed.'

Because of its central role in controlling the purse strings of the government, the Department of Public Expenditure and Reform (pronounced as 'Deeper' in government circles due to its acronym) can often feel like a clone of the government itself, with miniature versions of every other department nestled inside its own ('It's like a Russian doll,' says one TD; 'DPER has its own [Department of] Education, DPER has its own [Department of] Defence, everything'). Indeed, so careful is DPER in monitoring the broad handling of money that it is sometimes more on top of another department's affairs than that department's own minister.

'You would love to be ambitious and innovative in the way you shape your area,' says Richard Bruton, who led three departments at various times, 'but you find there are other commitments – things have been done that are impossible to undo – and you discover that your budgetary discretion is virtually tiny. You know, you're getting a six per cent increase in your budget, but when you go through it, it's all prior commitments, or commitments that have been made without a direct consideration of what the choices might be. And things can be happening with agencies and departments the minister doesn't know about.'

Bruton was seen as a more imaginative minister, never afraid to challenge departmental dogma – something which bore fruit when he was minister for jobs from 2011 to 2016, tasked with curbing rampant unemployment, but which chafed with establishment approaches in the Department of Education from 2016 to 2018, where teachers felt utterly overwhelmed by grand designs for reform. He found that DPER's default approach to budgeting – the conservative and perceivably prudent approach of copying and pasting last year's allocations as the starting point for the next year – can confound any appetite for real reform.

'DPER have very little appreciation for innovation. If you're trying to drive change, they will look at the existing system and its needs. They won't look at the potential for doing things differently. So, in the likes of [the Department of] Education, you have a much better chance of getting through, with DPER, a reduction of one in the pupil–teacher ratio, than […] creating a fund to promote innovation among the leadership of your primary schools. But if you ask which has the greater impact – reducing the pupil–teacher ratio by one, or spending money on innovation projects within schools, there's absolutely no contest. It's that sort of thing: there's embedded views of how public money gets spent, and they certainly don't engage in zero-based budgeting … the discretion that they will accept is within a very tight structure. And if you're trying to be innovative, or do new things, you'll be told, "Oh, no, yeah, you'll have to go to cabinet to get approval for a programme of that nature." It can be very frustrating.'

'I think in [the acronym] DPER, the "R" is being very generous to them.'

♟

Getting up and running as a minister of state can have its hiccups. Some departments receive junior ministers so regularly that offices are naturally set aside for them. Others receive them so sporadically, or in such variable number, that there isn't even an appropriate office to put them in. 'You'll want to be close to the senior minister's office,' says one, 'but they'll want to be close to their press people. Then you'll have people saying they'll take any auld office, and it doesn't matter what size it is – and someone else will intervene to say it has to be bigger, because if you're bringing people over from Europe you'll need to impress them.'

The relationships between senior and junior ministers in a department are regularly crucial, and can make or break the junior's career. Some departments are so large – Health is a common example – that the junior minister is presumed to have full political authority in a particular area, such as drugs strategy or mental health. In practice this authority is not always fully recognised by outside agencies or stakeholders. A junior minister being stymied by an unwilling agency might regularly need the senior to break down some doors for them.

The relationship can work both ways, however. A junior minister might be expected to take some of the burden in steering legislation through the Oireachtas, particularly at committee stage where bills get line-by-line scrutiny and amendments are considered. This creates a relationship that suits both: the junior can earn their stripes and claim some credit for whatever positive benefits come from their work, while the senior is spared some of the tedium of having to understand (and parlay) every jot and tittle of the bill before them. What's more, a junior minister might be able to fudge the question of whether to accept an opposition amendment put forward in good faith, knowing the senior minister has little or no appetite to take it on board. It's the classic 'good cop, bad cop' approach from Hollywood police dramas: one puts an acceptable face on the other's uncompromising nature.

Just as with cabinet-level ministries, in practical terms some junior ministries are more junior than others. There is the obvious hierarchy of departments and roles; the 'best' jobs are government chief whip, which comes with a seat at cabinet, or those with the perceived glamour of EU affairs. Both are attached to the Department of the Taoiseach, and come with visibility and exposure. Other jobs have less clout and don't entail any 'power' in a traditional sense: while some junior ministers are literally given delegated power from their senior counterpart, other roles simply don't have appropriate powers to warrant a delegation in the first place. A junior minister for the diaspora, for example, may be a nice spiritual envoy for the Irish overseas, but they will have no executive authority to do anything. In those cases the job can be what the minister makes of it. Some are happy to take the salary and plead powerlessness to do anything to justify it. Others try to look the part and treat it as an audition for the next big role.

'It's a "performance" job,' says one minister of state. 'The policy is not always yours and yours alone, so the job is to be a salesperson for it.'

This doesn't always go well. One former Fine Gael minister of state recalls a parliamentary party meeting where colleagues were lining up to criticise their senior minister, who was absent for an engagement in Brussels, about the practical impact of a new policy. The junior minister, feeling duty bound to defend the position of their absent master, volunteered to respond on their behalf – and was immediately met with a barrage of invective from colleagues who were quick to find a home for their ire.

Wounded, the junior minister later reported back to their senior minister about the oral beating dished out to them. That senior minister thanked them for their intervention – but calmly reminded them that, whatever about the substance of the reply, much of the opprobrium was likely to have been born from simple jealousy among others who envied the job.

§

When ministers reach the top of the tree, though, they can find themselves rather lonely looking down. It's a tall tree and the oxygen at the highest altitude is thinner than many had allowed for.

Eoghan Murphy was appointed minister for housing in 2017, having helped to steer Leo Varadkar through a Fine Gael leadership election and into the office of taoiseach – it was in Murphy's home that Varadkar conducted his tabletop geography exercise where the names of prospective ministers were written on ice cream sticks. Housing was a meaningful brief with scope to make advances, but became a different undertaking to that which Murphy had expected.

Having gone from the Public Accounts Committee to the Oireachtas Banking Inquiry, and then become a junior minister in the Department of Finance, Murphy had led a political life with a very fiscal outlook. A wide-ranging brief, with responsibility for everything from water supply to extreme weather and electoral management, would always have been a challenge. But two issues in particular stymied his progress, ultimately fatally.

The first was how the housing element of the portfolio quickly transformed from one of market management and intervention to one with a primarily social focus. Five months into his tenure, two people who had been sleeping rough were found dead in Dublin within just a few days of each other. 'I didn't have any experience with social issues – I just thought about numbers, and facts and figures – and all of a sudden I find myself in a brief that requires a great deal of empathy, and I can't give it, because I'm not used to giving it publicly. I don't think that was my only problem in Housing, but it was one of my problems in communication, because I wasn't used to it.'

The other problem was in overcoming the innate conservatism of the civil service around him. Two early projects Murphy wanted to push – a separate referendum on a constitutional right to housing, and a formal declaration of a housing 'emergency' in a bid to circumvent time-consuming planning procedures – were stymied by bureaucrats who saw limited benefits and larger pitfalls.

'A group of us, at the top of government, I see as having had our political careers forged post financial crisis, whether they were civil servants or politicians. And so, there was this conservatism around us, which completely disappeared by Covid-19. That conservativism kept us from escalating our response to housing. The ambition was there, the ideas were there, but we didn't actually respond to it at the level that we should have. And that's primarily my fault – because I'm the minister, I'm the person closest to it – but it's a collective responsibility as well, across the permanent government and the elected people, that we didn't treat it like Brexit, which […] we should have and we didn't.'

Eventually the public's perception of the portfolio as a social one, and Murphy's perception that the necessary urgency wasn't being shown by others, took a profound mental toll. Trying to convince others to show that urgency meant not just being able to sell the proposals, but to understand them at an intimate and intellectual level. That in turn meant late nights and weekends poring over briefing notes, with rarely any intellectual respite. That in turn meant trouble sleeping, and going to a multitude of doctors collecting various medications simply to chase any kind of restorative rest. All the while, passersby on the street would approach him and tell their kids that he was the man forcing children into homelessness.

By late 2019, after two and a half years in the role, Murphy wanted out. The number of people in emergency accommodation had surpassed 10,000, and a motion of no confidence – tantamount to the collapse of the cabinet – had been defeated only because three independent TDs had sided with the government. The housing situation was becoming problematic for the entire administration and Murphy's mental health was suffering. Had he been able to quit then, he would have, not merely as minister but as a TD entirely. He remained – not knowing that the government would effectively collapse a month later – because leaving would have damaged the cabinet as a whole.

By that time, Murphy says, 'I hated the job. I absolutely hated being in the public eye. I was getting way too much abuse. It wasn't worth it anymore … so it took a lot for me to run in that election. I let myself run, if you know what I mean – I let the momentum of what was coming carry me along, because I probably wasn't brave enough not to run.

'I got caught up in a kind of momentum. I got re-elected, which was hard for me to care about until I saw what it meant to my family and supporters that I hadn't quit, hadn't been kicked out, and stayed on to fight.

'But then, from that moment on, I was like, "Right, how soon can I leave?"'

Would he have felt differently if he had been appointed to a different job, a more spreadsheet-oriented brief like the Department of Enterprise? Maybe. In his role as a junior minister at the Department of Finance he had had engagements with the likes of the IDA and Enterprise Ireland, and the job might have been a more natural fit. But, Murphy says, had he been given a different job, his political career might have continued so long that it would have been impossible to walk away and pursue a separate career away from Leinster House afterwards. The bruising experience in the Department of Housing at least ended his ministerial career in time before he came too institutionalised to build a new life.

13

YES, TAOISEACH

An outsider might rationally think that cabinet-level ministers have a good perception of what the duties of a taoiseach entail. Those who eventually get the job, however, admit to being a little taken aback by just how differently the duties stack up.

For starters, the taoiseach might be elected to office on a groundswell of party and national support, but they're almost immediately dealing with enemies.

'It was one of the things I hated the most,' said Leo Varadkar, who had roles in the appointment of two cabinets. 'You're being made taoiseach, and everyone's happy for you and celebrating and all the rest – and the only thing you're thinking about is people you're going to disappoint or pass over, or make enemies of. And that's always the case. Nobody – no journalist ever – has ever written that a taoiseach got a reshuffle exactly right. There's things you always get wrong, which is why you usually try and avoid them.

'For every person you appoint, you've disappointed three or four others, and some of them might turn on you in the end.'

Simon Harris had been in cabinet for eight years before becoming Fine Gael leader, and taoiseach, in April 2024. 'The best description that a senior civil servant gave to me was: you think when you become taoiseach, you're going to become a kind of super-minister in charge of a really big department. But actually that's not what being taoiseach is at all: all of a sudden you're directly responsible for nothing, but you're actually responsible for everything.

'It's an entirely different skill set you need: your job, all of a sudden, is to bring people together, bang heads together, get people around a table to ask, "How are we going to fix this?" or "What do you think of that?". You're a convenor, and it's very different to the role of a minister.'

Varadkar, who served in the job twice, says the workload is technically infinite. 'It's like the scene from *Yes Minister*: there's the stuff you actually have to do, which is not enormous, but then there's the stuff that people expect you to do, and then the stuff that you want to do. When you add all that in, it's limitless.'

Academics like to sort different taoisigh into two categories: there are those who act like corporate chairs, scrutinising matters intently and continually trying to nudge others along from above; and then there are CEOs, who are more minded to roll their sleeves up and offer political backup (or pressure) to a minister who is struggling to register achievements in their roles.

Several ministers use different terminology to explain the differing approaches. 'There's a thing they say in rugby,' says one, 'that a good team has piano movers and piano players. Having someone who can play the piano in a concert hall is great, but you need a few people rolling their sleeves up to get the piano there in the first place.' Another uses a simpler sporting analogy: there are team managers, and there are team captains. The captain is influential but knows they are only one player on the team; the manager tries to imprint themselves on everything.

The distinction between chairs and CEOs, between piano movers and piano players, may become a more permanent feature of Irish politics if the largest parties all remain medium-sized in Dáil terms. It is in the nature of some people to act as CEOs, to be hands-on in leadership, to be the team managers, and to apply political pressure across government in getting things done – even if that means they are perceived as hogging the credit for other ministers' successes. Others excel in the arm's-length collegial approach, the captain on the field encouraging others to lift their game, and reaping reward from being the figurehead of an accomplished team of high performers.

One former colleague of Leo Varadkar's, for example, wonders if the composition of the three-party coalition played against his strengths. Becoming taoiseach in a minority government composed almost entirely of Fine Gael ministers – in the midst of national challenges like Brexit, which allowed the taoiseach to become a more active player – probably suited him, this minister says.

'Brexit was unusual because it gave Leo something to get his teeth into, which is unusual when the taoiseach is usually steering things from afar,' that minister says. 'Being able to go to [then-British prime minister] Boris Johnson, and thrash out a major compromise on the handling of the border, suited him down to the ground.

'Second time around, when he didn't have a big project – and he had to stay in his lane, pussy-footing around Fianna Fáil and the Greens in case he upset their ministers – was a totally different job. I don't think he understood, the second time, how much different it would be. I don't think it suited him at all.'

𝄢

However a taoiseach frames their own approach, one immediate piece of assistance in pursuing their agenda is that upon appointment, they get a much bigger personal team. Those who are taken aback by how small their core team is as a minister look on with envy at their boss: the taoiseach has a political staff of nine or ten, with a chief of staff, a full-time press secretary, and seven other political appointees – as well as private and personal secretaries to manage logistics, and a coterie of drivers and garda minders.

This, say onlookers, gives the taoiseach one advantage that other politicians don't have: sway. Of course there is a political authority from being at the top of the tree – and those with experience of working with them say the civil servants in the Department of the Taoiseach have a different temperament and tone to their work. The secretary general and the assistant secretaries have risen through the ranks partly because of political savviness: while not party political, they tend to be more capable as political operatives, and are better placed to put a taoiseach's sentiment into action. One former secretary general is purported to have told a then-taoiseach that, should the need arise, 'if the taoiseach says something, we can make it true' – not just as a political aspiration, but also as an insurance policy against gaffes.

But separately, the fleet of special advisors available to the taoiseach are able to follow up on issues that the time-pressed head of government simply cannot pursue themselves. If a special advisor acts as something of a proxy, a taoiseach can simply be in more places at once. (The European Commission has a *'cabinet'* system, where every member of the commission has their own personal team of executive political staff; those with experience of European politics think there is a lot to be said for similarly empowering the rest of the Irish cabinet, were it not for the fact that such a team would be visibly expensive to recruit.)

That ability to indirectly multitask is useful. The other thing that newcomers find in the office of taoiseach is quite how much travel they have to do. Meetings of the European Council of EU governmental leaders in Brussels, which were previously quarterly, now occur more frequently and in different configurations; there is a parallel 'European Political Community' gathering twice a year where non-EU leaders are also invited; an annual trip to the White House; the visit to Davos for the World Economic Forum; an annual *de facto* joint meeting of the British and Irish cabinets in March; attendance at the UN General Assembly in New

York in September, and the annual COP environmental summit in November, in whichever city is hosting. There is also often a long-distance trip scheduled for late July after the Dáil has risen for its summer break, perhaps to a strategic trade partner in Asia, or another trip back to North America to visit cities that couldn't be squeezed into the St Patrick's Day itinerary.

With all of that, the need to remain a visible and active presence in their own constituency, the weekly Tuesday-morning meeting of cabinet, and the expectation of being in the Dáil chamber for a couple of hours every Tuesday afternoon and Wednesday lunchtime, it can often feel like an achievement simply to attend a meeting.

The taoiseach's role as a coordinator-in-chief means much of the executive action is taken either via special advisors, via the media – announcing to the world that proposal X is unacceptable, and expecting others in government to take this as a public demarcation of priorities – or in cabinet subcommittees. Just as is the case with government departments, a new taoiseach has the freedom to restructure and redesign committees howsoever they like (though their makeup is often influenced by the *realpolitik* of the Programme for Government, and the various configurations in which the taoiseach needs to steer the unwieldy machinery of government).

Those who participate in cabinet subcommittees say that they have two upsides: the first is that, unlike the standard Tuesday-morning meeting of the full cabinet, subcommittees often happen on low-profile Thursday afternoons – without a small cabal of TV cameras and reporters camped outside the gates. While ministers are often capable of blocking out the exterior noise of media speculation, nonetheless there are times when outside media pressure – or briefings to reporters by opponents on an issue – can unnerve those inside the room. (Some ministers cite the 2020 decision to defy the public health advice, and allow households to mingle indoors while also reopening pubs in the run-up to Christmas, as an example of bowing to public pressure instead of making the 'correct' call.) Allowing meetings to take place with no specific prior advertising or without a major discussion point on the agenda, participants say, can allow for more open and constructive discussion.

Secondly, whereas everyday junior ministers only attend meetings when strictly needed (for example, a junior minister for enterprise or finance may be asked to present an item relating to their specific brief), they are regular attendees of subcommittees. The cabinet subcommittee on European matters, for example, would routinely include the presence of the junior minister specialising on EU affairs; in previous governments the subcommittee on health would include not just the senior minister for health but all three or four of their junior ministers.

The downside, as those participants see it, is that the meetings can be few and far between. It is common for a cabinet subcommittee to go for a couple of months without a meeting, due to pressures on the taoiseach's diary and the perception that other matters are more worthy of immediate attention.

It is worth putting on the record that there is a conceptual vagueness about the status of subcommittees and the presence of junior ministers. Are these get-togethers literal subcommittees of the cabinet proper and, if so, are ministers of state *actually* entitled to be considered 'members'? There are some who take the view that, given the constitutional requirement for contributions at cabinet to be kept confidential among members, even the standard presence of having three select 'super juniors' at its weekly meetings is a legal no-no. Enda Kenny's subcommittees considered the junior health ministers to be full members, for example, but Leo Varadkar's merely described them as being 'invited' to show up.

There are broader points too: the Monday-night meetings of the Fianna Fáil/Fine Gael/Green leaders during their 2020–2025 coalition, which acted as a clearing house for any cabinet business and a forum through which inevitable rows could be defused or deferred, were described on the Dáil record as a 'committee on cabinet coordination' with only those three figures as members. Yet, as a matter of fact, the three leaders' individual chiefs of staff were also weekly attendees at those meetings. If a junior minister can't attend a cabinet committee, why can a non-office-holder do so? And if those meetings are tantamount to subgroups of cabinet, are they immune from Freedom of Information requests in the same way that 'regular' cabinet meetings are impregnable to outside inquiry?

In any event, not everyone is impressed with the structure of subcommittees anyway. One former minister sees them as a double-edged sword: 'If you can really convince the taoiseach of the need for action, you come away emboldened – as the saying goes, you can bite with the president's teeth. But otherwise the meetings often don't have a specific agenda, or there is no overarching long-term goal. You end up getting into a room, hoping the taoiseach will knock heads or order action on something. If you can't get him on board, you end up just having a check-in and you don't come away with any points of action. In an ideal world you'd have broader strategic objectives. What you end up getting is navel-gazing.'

With the benefit of hindsight, some of the more frugal measures adopted during the era of austerity were penny wise, pound foolish. The abolition of state cars and garda drivers for most cabinet members – saving about €2.5 million a year, mostly by freeing up garda time – was a visible gesture of frugality from ministers who knew the public would demand some token of sacrifice from those who were better off.

Scaling back the use of the government jets, however, may have been a little more unwise. It was true that a seat in economy class on a flight to Brussels was far cheaper than the nominal €4,940 hourly cost of using the government jet, but an unexpected downside was that cabinet members no longer had any privacy on the plane. 'You'd be sitting there going over to Brussels for a Council [of the European Union] meeting,' one former special advisor recalls, 'and the minister would be scared to open their briefing notes, in case there was something sensitive that the person sitting next to them would be able to read.' In one instance a minister's notes were reconstituted as soggy bumf when the passenger sitting beside them spilled a drink during a moment of turbulence.

Another sacrifice was the decision not to commission a new Gulfstream jet when the existing one fell into disrepair in 2014. The larger of the government's two aircraft, the Gulfstream was the only one with adequate range to bring a minister to the east coast of the United States – it was this plane that would ordinarily carry the taoiseach to Washington for the engagements around St Patrick's Day, for example. Flying transatlantic on a regular Aer Lingus service was hardly much of an imposition, and a new protocol would still allow ministers to fly in business class if their schedule of engagements required them to arrive refreshed upon landing. Internal flights on such visits, however, were a different proposition. The author has firsthand experience of seeing Enda Kenny, having tried valiantly to grab an hour of sleep in the aisle seat of a late-night internal flight, being unmercifully hoofed awake by the clatter of a drinks trolley striking his shoulder.

Another accidental consequence was increasing reliance on the smaller Learjet, which still remained in use for shorter-term journeys that could not be made on commercial flights. It too began to show disrepair, and would increasingly leave a taoiseach or tánaiste stranded in a European capital, capable of making one leg of the journey, but suffering any number of mechanical faults before the return leg. This jet was eventually also put out of its misery, but a replacement jet only arrived after senior ministers sank over €1 million into the hire of private jets as 'air taxis' in 2024.

That said, those with the pleasure of travelling on the ministerial air fleet quickly forget how much easier it is than commercial flying. One member of ministerial staff became so accustomed to the ease of business travel – a Garda escort could bring them from the offices on Merrion Street to the military aerodrome at Baldonnell, and into the air, within 30 minutes – that they simply forgot what it was like having to fly commercially. The next time they had to drag their young children on a commercial flight from Dublin Airport, they resolved simply to take the ferry in future.

14

THE LOBBYISTS IN THE LOBBY

It is said that anyone on the planet can be connected to anyone else through six degrees of separation: person A is known to B, who is friends with C, who is colleagues with D, and so on. Though there can be no empirical proof of this, politicians will commonly believe that Ireland is a much more efficient place in which to find connections. Often politicians simply find they can get things done, and find doors opening for them, because the nature of their job requires them to be as open and personable as possible. The more people they meet, the more they know; the more they know, the wider their sphere of influence.

The same can be true outside Leinster House. Those who know more of the cast of characters inside the gates are more likely to feel they can gain the inside track, or perhaps ask a favour here and there. Much of this is innocent – former staff getting in touch with remaining colleagues asking about the status of something; a former journalist asking for a phone number – but some make a business of monetising that influence.

Despite the baggage that comes with the term, most lobbying of Oireachtas members is mundane at best. 'It's a bit of a chore,' says a government backbencher. 'Of course you'd be polite and listen, and be thoughtful, but you're attending meetings that wouldn't make much difference to your outlook. And, to be honest, you'd be better off directing the arguments to the minister anyway.'

Lobbying in Ireland is simultaneously regulated by law and utterly ungovernable. 'What even is lobbying?' asks one TD, reasonably. 'Yes, a trade union or a business group asking for a new policy is definitely lobbying. But if an employee, or an employer, speaks to me and suggests a change in law, is that lobbying?' As they see it, the pursuit is the same, and the only difference is formality.

Since 2015, there is a certain transparency to lobbying in Ireland – at least in its professional incarnation. Bodies seeking to influence governmental thinking, or changes in the law, are required to register with the Standards in Public Office Commission (SIPO) and make almost real-time disclosures about any sort of contact they strive to establish. This applies to almost any interaction, from a formal face-to-face meeting with a TD or minister to a mere email that does not even require a reply.

This comprehensive requirement was designed partly to ensure that transparency was not only achieved, but seen to be achieved. After the tribunals that dominated political life in the 1990s and 2010s, politicians wanted to be perceived as being beyond reproach. Those who serve today aren't convinced the legislation has achieved that goal.

'It's overkill,' says one politician. 'The transparency is fine but it's actually too much. If you go to the website and search for my name, you'll see so many people saying they've lobbied me that you'd struggle to pick out the ones who have met me to my face.'

Others have a more generous outlook on it. 'Everyone thinks we're all crooked,' says a senator. 'The only way to convince people otherwise is to prove it.'

Whether the 2015 laws have sanitised the lobbying trade remains open to question. Those laws require anyone considered a 'designated public official' – any minister, TD, MEP, councillor or special advisor, as well as the highest grade of civil servants – to observe a cooling-off period before they can engage in lobbying. Rather than saying goodbye to colleagues on a Friday and then contacting them as lobbyists the next Monday, practitioners are required by law to spend 12 months out of action or working in some other field. This also doesn't mean the person can join a lobbying company and direct matters from farther afield: the law even goes so far as to say they cannot work for an organisation engaged in lobbying.

But how robust is this rule? Not terribly. SIPO can grant exemptions from the cooling-off period, without being forced to name the person who has received it or the reason they've got it. It is presupposed that some got an exemption because the job being offered to them was only vacant for a short period – a 'use it or lose it' kind of situation. The truth of this is hard to ascertain: if a former political insider has valuable access to the corridors of power today, the chances are that they'd still be an equally attractive candidate at the other end of their mandatory quarantine. One regular stipulation of these cooling-off exemptions is that, while the lobbyist is free to work in most areas, they agree not to engage in any direct approaches to their former department or the people who worked there.

Moreover, the cooling-off period has been notoriously difficult to enforce: when sitting senator Michael D'Arcy quit the Seanad to become the chair of the Irish Association of Investment Managers, it emerged that there was no sanction in law for anyone who simply ignored the cooling-off window. D'Arcy's case was especially sensitive as he had previously been a junior minister responsible for the regulation of the funds industry, and was now becoming the head of the representative group for fund managers. (For the record, there is no evidence of D'Arcy having engaged in any lobbying for that year.) Only in 2023 was the law updated to include a sanction for those who engaged in lobbying before the expiry of the 12-month period.

The departure of a sitting Oireachtas member to become a lobbyist, however indirectly, illustrates the extent of the revolving door within the lobbying sector in Ireland. It stands to reason that those with the most experience of how inner government works might be the ones best able to influence it from the outside. This influence can be wielded not just by politicians themselves, but equally by their former advisors. It is partly for this reason that so many politicians, and the staff who work for them, can be in high demand when their full-time stay in Leinster House has come to an end.

An analysis by TheJournal.ie in 2022 revealed that 62 special advisors appointed since 2011 had subsequently engaged in lobbying activity on behalf of private clients. The number has definitively grown since then, given the general rotation of ministers in and out of office, and the revolving door of staff who go in and out in their wake.

In some instances, the lobbyist will be a former employee of the minister themselves. One is Feargal Purcell, who served as government press secretary under Enda Kenny and for a brief period under Leo Varadkar. Purcell was granted a cooling-off exemption to become a public affairs consultant at the communications firm Edelman, and is recorded as having lobbied Varadkar as taoiseach on a few occasions since then. One phone call was on behalf of Airbnb, ascertaining whether his former boss might be available to meet with the company's CEO to discuss the value of the short-term lettings sector to Irish tourism. Considering that the short-term lettings sector has also been blamed for the chronic shortage of housing in the long-term rental market, it was a sensitive topic to broach. Airbnb's own head of public affairs might have been able to make the approach himself: the job was held at the time by Derek Nolan, a former coalition colleague of Varadkar who had been a Labour TD on the government backbenches from 2011 to 2016.

Another such lobbyist is Stephen Lynam, who joined the public affairs firm Q4 after his time working as a special advisor for Paschal Donohoe, and then found himself lobbying Donohoe on behalf of many corporate clients. Lynam is not unique: Q4 is such a prominent firm in the Dublin public affairs and public relations scene that its employees, and those of other large firms, can have a two-way relationship with politics – not only do former advisors join them, but their own staff can be poached as special advisors. Páraic Gallagher joined Q4 after a distinguished career in radio journalism but was subsequently approached by Stephen Donnelly to become his special advisor – and was promptly lobbied by some of his former colleagues.

Sometimes individual personnel end up moving in both directions: there are a few documented cases of former advisors who have joined such firms and worked alongside people who used to lobby them, and then gone back into government roles after a change of ministerial personnel. There are other cases where officials in a department move into more senior roles in other agencies and find themselves being lobbied by people they first knew as special advisors to the ministers with whom they worked in their old jobs.

'Your phone is always busy,' says one minister. 'It stands to reason that if you see a text or a phone call from a name you recognise, you're more likely to look at it properly – even if it's to see if they're ringing to tell you someone is after dying.'

⚷

In the course of researching this book, the author asked many Oireachtas members if they had been the targets of lobbying. Many replied to the effect of 'not really'. When the entries to the lobbying register were read to them, they were a little taken aback. Not all of the lobbying even entailed direct contact. Some of it was merely a demonstration arranged outside Leinster House – a staged photo opportunity at the Kildare Street gates – which was directed at those politicians but wasn't necessarily on their radar. So comprehensive is the register that most interest groups believe they have to disclose the target of their campaigning, even if the target doesn't directly engage with it.

Often the contact is a little more mundane and relates to someone's position on an Oireachtas committee, or simply because they're a member of the same party as a government minister. Every single Green TD and senator, for example, might get an email from an environmentalist group looking for more affirmative action to cut carbon emissions. Every Dubliner in Leinster House might get a letter from a group seeking a review of proposed transport options. Everyone on the Joint Oireachtas Committee on Education could get a call to their office about the shortage of training spaces in a certain discipline.

One grey area for the recipients of lobbying concerns what passes the threshold for being registered and what doesn't. One informant gives the example of a concerned citizen who wants to email a minister about something on their mind. Those with a better understanding of the legislative procedure might email every member of the appropriate committee. That's self-evidently not lobbying: it's a citizen engaging in the democratic process. But say that citizen shares their views online, rallies other people to their view, and they end up forming an *ad-hoc* campaign group. Does this count as a group for the purposes of regulation? What if a single person creates an online template through which Oireachtas members receive multiple copies of the same stock email? The legislation doesn't consider this as lobbying activity – it is framed as applying only to professional lobbyists, those who engage in public affairs for a living – despite occasions where this campaigning is more politically potent than a genteel handshake from a former colleague. Nonetheless many entries on the register of lobbying pertain to voluntary groups.

Other professional lobby groups disclose contact with politicians that they haven't even initiated themselves. It's routine for such groups to hold press conferences in Buswells Hotel, just across the street from the Kildare Street gates to Leinster House. If an Oireachtas member drops by and is thus present to hear the case being advocated, groups feel compelled to include this as an act of lobbying. A small informal hello after the event is likewise disclosed. If TDs' offices have been emailed to let them know of the event, and those offices reply with even a courtesy acknowledgement of the invite, that too gets disclosed.

ฦ

A double-edged sword for many serving Oireachtas members is the fact that former TDs and senators retain the privilege of life-long access to Leinster House, the opportunity to avail of free car parking on the grounds, and even the right to visit the members' bar and restaurants. This applies even to the shortest-serving parliamentarians, 'weekend senators' who are appointed to vacant seats on an outgoing lame-duck Seanad, often as a ceremonial honour by a gratefully re-elected taoiseach.

There are not many examples of these privileges being used for nefarious purposes, however. 'If someone wanted to meet me,' says one TD, 'there'd be no need for them to wander in and try to snare me in the corridor. This job is wall-to-wall with meetings, why would you not ask for one?' Another is still more unsympathetic and believes an unsolicited visitor to Leinster House would do more harm than good to their cause. Someone with a reputation for hanging around uninvited, they think, would only end up aggravating the very people they're supposed to be winning over.

There may be a perception that lobbying is the last stronghold of corporate influence on Irish politics, and that in an era of almost zero tolerance on corporate donations, it's the only meaningful way for commercial influences to exert their sway on the democratic process. This may be true in a functional sense, but most politicians do not see it as a purely negative aspect of how policy is formed and how decisions are reached. That's not to say the view is a universal one: quite a few TDs, especially those on the left, do perceive the role of outside interests as corrosive to the national interest. (They may, in turn, be less likely to receive submissions: a search for two members of the Oireachtas Committee on Climate Action shows the more overtly left TDs are simply less targeted by lobbyist approaches than centre-left colleagues on the same committee.)

Some others, however, seem sanguine – or at least reluctantly accepting – about the role of lobbyists in general, seeing them as a simple necessity for movements or enterprise bodies to communicate their views on the issues of the day. Though it may not be the most strictly democratic means of engagement, and elevates the 'haves' above the 'have-nots', it at least provides a forum for outside views to be heard.

All politicians, ultimately, are wary of inhabiting ivory towers. The difference is merely their view on whether lobbyists are fellow dwellers of the same ivory towers, or whether they might have tapped into a public concern that the politicians themselves have not picked up on.

'It's not exactly dark arts,' concludes one. 'All they're doing is making a case. It's up to politicians to decide whether to act.'

15

THE HOLIEST OF HOLIES

It is perhaps the most-talked-about watering hole in the country; rumours abound about the low price of its drinks and the exalted company there. There are no photographs of this paradise of secrecy; its existence is so wrapped up in fable that even those who have been there are known to joke about whether it exists at all.

So what exactly is the Dáil bar like?

Firstly, a note of clarification. There are, in fact, two bars: one much more secretive and exclusive than the other. Any visitor to Leinster House can be brought to the 'Strangers' Bar', an almost mandatory stop on any tour of Leinster House. Touring groups of senior citizens and schoolchildren are routinely brought there for a glass of wine or a soft drink (respectively, usually) and perhaps a bag of crisps. Staff from the complex might pop in for lunch; the soup and toasted sandwiches are particular favourites of many. Interns might be brought in by politicians on their last day for a valid knees-up. Journalists may toast the appointment or departure of a colleague with a few pints after their respective deadlines. The decor is clean but unremarkable, with sturdy wooden furnishings and a suspended ceiling to mask the industrial feel of the overhead roof windows. Picture a brightly lit bar in a provincial hotel and you wouldn't be far off, except the televisions only show live feeds of the two parliamentary chambers.

Then, in an adjoining room, there is (reportedly, at least) a mirror image of the same bar, connected by a single internal door allowing the bar staff to easily skip from one to the other. This is the members' bar, *the* Dáil bar, one of the most exclusive drinking establishments in the country. Only members of the Oireachtas themselves, past and present, are allowed to set foot inside the door. While members can bring outside guests into the equivalent members' restaurant on the same corridor, the bar is the holiest of holies: only people who have had the words 'Deputy' or 'Senator' attached to their names are permitted inside the door. So secretive is it that even passing by on the corridor – beneath a sign that simply says *Private* – there is no way to peep inside: if the door is swinging open, all that can be seen is a small anteroom with a perfunctory table and chair.

Cosmetically, the members' bar is a little more colourful than its less secretive twin. The walls are festooned with pictures of Oireachtas sporting groups – prize-winners at a golf society event; rugby teams that faced off against inter-parliamentary rivals on the weekend of a Six Nations match – and additional flat screens where members can watch horse racing or some other live sport as well as the proceedings in the Dáil or Seanad. At the back is a door to a small, secluded outdoor smoking area, where politicians can puff in peace, in the not-quite-luxurious surrounds of a former industrial service area.

Back inside, the parallels with a slightly snobby secondary school once again come to the fore: given the high-powered nature of the clientele, the institution is surprisingly cliquish. Through long-standing custom the biggest parties have *de facto* areas of their own, where it is regularly understood that (say) only Fianna Fáil politicians will sit, and where it would be taboo for infidels of any other party to join them. One TD, searching for an explanatory comparison, likens it to the high-school canteen in *Mean Girls*.

Not only that, but the comparably egalitarian approaches to business in the canteens are dispensed with. Should they venture in for a sup, cabinet ministers enjoy seniority, and more junior

TDs within their ranks are only accepted in the same company by invitation. 'If the taoiseach is in there, sitting at a table, under no circumstances do you plonk yourself down on a seat beside him,' says one. 'If he calls you over and invites you down, go ahead, but otherwise keep to your own company and don't bother him.'

§

It ought to be noted that during daytime the bar is generally quiet. Contrary to widespread belief, it is not especially cheap: prices in the members' bar are the same as in the strangers' bar on the other side of the wall, and are only moderately cheaper than any other Dublin pub. (Like the restaurants, the bars are not specifically money-making vehicles, and property costs do not have to be factored into their prices.)

The busiest period is around lunch, when many members may drop in for soup or a panini, or can ask the staff to bring whatever joint of the day is being served in the adjoining public canteen. Tuesday and Wednesday evenings can be busier: Wednesdays because that's usually when parliamentary party meetings take place, and when the Dáil holds its usual voting session; Tuesdays because members from outside Dublin simply have few other venues to pass the time. Being just across a corridor from one entrance to the Dáil chamber – and far, far closer to the chamber than the personal offices of most members – it is a natural hangout for deputies who don't plan on speaking in a debate but who need to stay nearby for eventual votes.

Because the bar exists in something of a legal void – being a members' club, it doesn't have to apply to a court for a licence, or observe the same fixed hours as most pubs – it can also remain open late, at least as long as there are people to serve. On a typical night, the bar remains open for half an hour after business in the Dáil and Seanad chambers has wrapped up, in practice meaning it is regularly open until after midnight on the Wednesday of a sitting week. (Those who want to stay out any later will regularly decamp to the various bars of Dawson Street.)

The fact that the bar is next door to the chamber – and will serve its members so long as the Houses are in session – means that when emotive legislation is debated into the evening and overnight, the blood alcohol levels of politicians often rise accordingly. This does not mean that every politician gets drunk; some Leinster House lifers insist they have only ever seen one instance of a politician being visibly intoxicated (for whom the corrective action was a colleague shepherding them to their hotel in a taxi).

One well-known example of alcoholic influence on proceedings was in 2013, when the Fine Gael–Labour coalition had proposed laws seeking to regularise access to abortion in line with the 1992 Supreme Court ruling in the 'X' Case. (The court had declared that abortion in Ireland could be permissible if continuing the pregnancy threatened the life of the mother, but in the intervening 20 years, no government had ever introduced laws to give this a practical grounding.)

As is often the case, the government whips had naïvely underestimated how much time would be needed to let the debate run its course, and having originally been planned to finish at midnight, on some evenings the debate continued until 5 a.m., the bar remaining open for its illustrious clientele all the while. Members in the chamber recalled how the debate itself was becoming harder and harder to hear over the din of chatter from slightly inebriated members who thought they were whispering to each other. In a 5 a.m. vote one TD, visibly worse for wear, voted against their party's position on a particularly emotive amendment. Ordinarily, breaking the party whip would result in a suspension from membership of that party. In that instance, the party whip simply declared the vote to be an error and a blind eye was turned.

The high-water mark – or lowest ebb, depending on your per-suasion – came after one vote had been called at 2:40 a.m., and members were milling about in the chamber. Fine Gael TD Tom Barry, sitting in the seat he would occupy for the electronic vote, pulled party colleague Áine Collins onto his lap. An unimpressed Collins politely, but firmly, rose back to her feet and brushed herself down. On another occasion, the incident might have gone unnoticed, but such was the sensitive and high-profile nature of the debate that TV3 had left the Dáil's proceedings broadcasting live on air overnight, and the incident was spotted by a viewer who posted the clip online in near real time, sending it viral, making international news on CNN and Sky as well as at home. Mortified both by his own actions and the international disrepute, Barry offered to resign as a TD, an offer rebuffed by then-taoiseach Enda Kenny. Others simply digested the incident as a cautionary tale and scaled back their weeknight intake.

ß

There is no doubt that Leinster House was, for previous political generations, an astonishingly boozy workplace. Until the middle of the 2010s, the business of the Dáil was structured in such a way that votes could be held at relatively short notice. TDs in a government with a narrow majority did not have the latitude to leave the premises, because depending on the topic being discussed, or the legislation being debated, multiple votes could be demanded in quick succession. The bars, barely 30 seconds' walk from the closest door to the chamber, made for a convenient base in between. Almost by default, members who could be hovering for hours waiting for a series of votes would end up in the bar, simply biding their time until the division bell rang once again.

One TD with experience of the bar in the early, and later, parts of the decade cringes when recalling the booziness. 'If you think of the other TDs as being like classmates, we'd end up on the beer on a Tuesday night, and again on a Wednesday, and then at weekends I'd end up having to go out with friends at home. Before knowing it, I'd be on a session three or four nights a week, and trying to be a TD in the middle of it all. It was impossible to keep it all up.'

Some put a more modern culture of moderation down to the Barry incident in 2013, dubbed 'Lapgate' in the media. Others believe the consequences of the 2016 election had a part to play: firstly in the rearrangement of Dáil schedules so that spontaneous votes were few and far between; and secondly, because of a quirk in how committee seats are filled. While the distribution of seats on committees is proportional to the seats in the Dáil itself, ministers are not able to serve as committee members, leaving government backbenchers stretched slightly more thinly to make up the numbers. Of the 50 Fine Gael TDs elected in 2016, 28 became ministers of one sort or another, leaving the other 22 to share the workload commensurate with 50 seats. Suddenly TDs who had become accustomed to drinking at work simply hadn't the time for a pint any more. Some who lived through that era, while acknowledging that their admission is slightly embarrassing, will confess to feeling sorry for their younger colleagues who never got to 'enjoy' the bar to the same degree as their older peers.

Whatever the reason, the workplace is not nearly as boozy as it once was, and Wednesday nights are now the only evening on which a decent crowd can be expected.

ȣ

Many readers might understandably bristle at the idea of any workplace – let alone the one that sets rules for the rest of society – having its own in-house bar. Many politicians agree: none of the above should be interpreted as saying the bars in Leinster

House are a universal hangout. Quite a few of them, approached for some insights when writing this chapter, swore they'd never been inside it. Many others have been in for a bowl of soup for lunch, but rarely darken its door on an evening.

A counterpoint was offered by a small number of TDs whose careers have included needing to weather intense moments of controversy or even crisis. For them, a private bar is an indispensable sanctuary in times of acute strife.

'If you're in the middle of a shitstorm,' one says, 'you can't just rock up in your local at home and pretend everything's grand. You only need one eejit to start having a go with you, and the night's over. And they don't even need to say anything to your face; they can just tell their WhatsApp group that yer man the TD is in the pub, and someone else will come in and give you grief. At least in the members' bar you know who you're going to see, and the company you're going to keep.'

16

A CAST OF THOUSANDS

The Leinster House complex is the daily workplace for about 1,200 people. Despite its being the epicentre of Irish politics, politicians themselves only make up a fraction of its daily inhabitants. Sharing the workplace is an enormous coterie of advisors, staff, secretariats, ushers, administrators and other legions of hangers-on.

The biggest portion of staff are those attached to TDs and senators themselves: every member of the Oireachtas is granted a secretarial assistant (or at least an allowance for one), while TDs are also given a parliamentary assistant to deal with the management of their daily duties.

Ask any politician how they would survive without their support staff, and you will receive a universal refrain: without them, simply put, nothing would be done. Even lifers in Leinster House are utterly reliant on their staff for everyday tasks. 'I'm here a while now,' says one veteran, 'and I will admit that I have no idea where I would get a box of envelopes from. I'm so wrapped up in constituency work that I genuinely wouldn't know who to ring or what door to knock on.' One only discovered the extent of their true reliance on their staff when they received a call from a school principal looking to confirm their booking of a school tour visit, on a week when an office staff member was on leave. 'I knew you had to clear any visitors with the head usher's office, but I had no idea how to contact them. My staff were the mediators for everything.'

Despite their importance to the political operation, the staff attached to politicians are not especially well paid. Parliamentary assistants, who often find themselves acting as proxy TDs given the administrative and practical workload, and who often work the same long hours as the TDs themselves, have a starting salary of €43,767, lower than the average national full-time wage and significantly lower than that of most full-time workers in Dublin. Administrative assistants' salaries start on €36,854. The latter is a significant improvement on an older system, phased out only in 2022, where the title was merely that of 'secretarial assistant' and the pay began at around €24,400. Given these were the only staff available to senators, who would otherwise have been running offices entirely alone, many senators would subtly talk up the experience or qualifications of their appointees so that the new hire could start at a mildly higher point on the salary scale and eke out a tenable existence in Dublin.

The jobs can be especially thankless because of the inflexible working hours. Officially speaking, the positions come with a 40-hour working week, with the possibility of being paid extra for overtime. 'Possibility' is the crucial word here, as in practical terms being able to vouch for extra time worked is a persistent challenge. Parliamentary assistants might see it as their duty to hang around the building for as long as their masters are occupied with Dáil business. On a Wednesday night, when votes usually take place, for example, the Dáil might only finish up after 11 p.m., having begun its day just after 9 a.m. that morning – and members might be due back in for question time at 9 a.m. the next day. As these are all sitting hours, and core to the functioning of the Dáil, they do not count as 'overtime'. As one assistant explains it, even legitimate overtime claims – which are limited to eight hours per week – often only scratch the surface of the workload. 'If I get a press query or a message from a journalist at 10 p.m. on a Sunday night – which happens – and I respond or even read it,' says one, 'what price do you put on that?'

Parliamentary assistants have been known to use their access to pursue causes of their own, often as supplements to those of the politician they serve, and never to the detriment of whatever agenda the politician is themselves pursuing. One way they do so is by tabling written Parliamentary Questions (or 'PQs' in Leinster House jargon) in the name of their politician, sometimes completely of their own volition, sometimes upon suggestion from a journalist with a shared concern. This results in the TD receiving an on-the-record response from the minister, tantamount to a written declaration of policy or the disclosure of new information, without the TD ever knowing anything about it. 'Once or twice I have got phone calls from journalists asking me what I thought about the minister's reply to my PQ,' admits one deputy, 'and I've had to lie and say I hadn't actually seen the reply yet, and told them I'd ring them back when I'd had a chance to read it. The PQ was actually put in by my staff – on an issue I would care about, but just hadn't acted on – but I knew absolutely nothing about it.'

This is an innocuous example, but there have been times when politicians have risked placing too much authority and trust in the hands of their staff. Independent TDs are particularly reliant on their staff to act as speechwriters: whereas formal political parties usually have spokespersons on specific matters, who will take the lead speaking in appropriate debates, independents have no such division of labour and will want to speak themselves on almost any issue of relevance to their area. Scripts for these speeches are often produced at arm's length from the TD, who has little or no opportunity to scrutinise the text before delivering it in the Dáil. Many of those staff will themselves have no specialised experience in the specific area under discussion, and might start drafting a speech by copying the remarks of whichever minister sponsored the bill being discussed, and substituting each point with counterpoints as they go. This is an efficient method of speechwriting when it works, but a dangerous one when it doesn't: at least once, rushed or careless drafting has left a TD unknowingly delivering a speech that makes arguments on both sides of a debate, faithfully parroting a government argument in one breath and sincerely arguing against it in the next.

More than one politician interviewed for this book raised concerns that the churn of speechwriting was inadvertently laundering fake news by giving it a parliamentary platform. The scenario portrayed by one was as follows: a constituent with an axe to grind calls up the office to vent about a chosen topic, an inexperienced staff member takes the claim at face value, includes it as an anecdote in a speech they're drafting without being able to vouch for its veracity, and eventually has the story repeated in the Dáil with the benefit of parliamentary privilege and a veneer of authority. 'You see some TDs standing up and complaining about the behaviour of asylum-seekers, or what have you, with no idea if it's actually true,' one believes, concerned that the floor of the Dáil is being used to legitimise hearsay with no factual basis.

Another is convinced that a fellow politician gave a speech written by ChatGPT, the artificial intelligence program with a known tendency to 'hallucinate' fictitious answers to questions. This TD's belief is that the politician concerned, looking for help to draft a speech about an international event, supplied ChatGPT with a prompt premised on a wrongful and skewed interpretation of actual events. As ChatGPT works off a finite data set, and cannot react to ongoing contemporary events, the program would not only have accepted the wrongful premise in good faith, but possibly compounded the problem by introducing fresh (fictional) angles of supposed argument. This theory cannot be proven for certain, but ChatGPT's output for a similarly erroneous request is not a million miles away from some of what now appears on the Oireachtas record.

ß

Within Leinster House, the arrangement of offices can be instructive about the relationship between a TD and their staff. The majority of TDs have offices in the LH2000 Block, a millennium-era development which includes the Oireachtas' four main committee rooms as well as a multistorey office block. The offices there are partitioned, with an inner and outer office. Most politicians take the inner office for themselves, and leave their two staff sharing the smaller outer space – the sort of arrangement you might imagine in a corporate setting, with a CEO in the inner office and a receptionist or secretary as the gatekeeper. This sensibility is mortifying to others, who take the smaller workspace for themselves, and allow their two support staff to work in the larger inner space. Those politicians find themselves, in effect, working out of the anteroom of their own office.

Splitting the duties of the two staff can itself be thorny. As the title and pay grades would suggest, the administrative assistant's job is primarily to manage the clerical workload, keeping an eye on the inbox during the day and shuttling constituency inquiries between constituents and state bodies. A parliamentary assistant's job is inherently to be more political, liaising on committee work, drafting speeches, pitching policy ideas, drafting press releases and the like. For this team of three, a natural sense of collegiality might set in, a sense of 'we're all in this together' and a natural splitting of workloads. One deputy consciously cultivated this spirit with his staff, hoping that the camaraderie of the workplace would breed some kind of synergy and a desire from each worker to feel duty to the other. The system worked for a few months, until the lesser-paid secretarial assistant (as the job was then called, with the lower pay to match) abruptly walked out. Being asked to take on extra and more meaningful responsibilities was rewarding, they explained, but their morale was irreparably ruined when the penny dropped that the parliamentary assistant was earning many more pennies for what, in practice, was the same work.

Those occasional mishaps aside, the staff are simply indispensable to an ambitious TD's operation. David Cullinane said his Sinn Féin blueprint for the 2024 election – which he hoped would become the basis for a programme for government, were Sinn Féin to enter power – was written entirely by himself and his parliamentary assistant, who had spent two years engaging with stakeholders looking to figure out a workable and deliverable plan. The job was an enormous task for two people, he said, but would have been impossible for someone working alone.

And at the crucial crunch moments, the staff are there. Many TDs speak of the weight of responsibility they feel as polling closes in an election and the staff, through no failing of their own, have put their own jobs in jeopardy.

'I remember standing in my kitchen as the polls closed,' says one TD of the 2020 election, 'and it suddenly hit me that there were two other people facing the abyss. My partner was working, and our own severance payments are decent if we have to go.' (A TD elected before 2012 can claim their parliamentary pension from the age of 50; newer TDs can still receive severance payments worth up to €71,000 depending on their length of service.) 'So I'd be fine – but there were two other people whose entire livelihood depended on me getting elected. I nearly threw up.'

ʠ

Irrespective of one's status or rank, any visitor to Leinster House will come across two categories of staff without whom Leinster House couldn't function at all.

The first is the catering team, led by long-standing stalwart Julie Lyons, that keeps the place fed and watered. Julie's kitchen team produces the lunches and dinners eaten by most of the 1,200-or-so staff in the building every day. The hot dinners are lapped up with gusto by everyone from cabinet ministers to office staff. Even as taoiseach, Simon Harris has been known to keep up his habit of getting his hot lunch in the self-service canteen. So frequent a visitor is he that on his thirty-eighth birthday – his first as taoiseach – Julie and company made him a personalised cake. Harris is not unique in being a regular visitor: Enda Kenny was also a frequent diner there, including on the day that Leo Varadkar succeeded him as taoiseach. This author personally witnessed Kenny's meat-and-two-veg lunch going cold as he received congratulatory well wishes, while Varadkar was receiving his seal of office 20 minutes' drive away.

Micheál Martin had less time to visit for lunch while he was in the taoiseach's office; previously, however, he would frequently stop by the salad bar for a light meal. Martin is a notoriously parsimonious eater, always watching out for excess calories. One evening on an election trail he admonished a journalist who he spotted eating a takeaway during a hurried meal break. A few weeks later the same journalist spotted him in the canteen and was keen to point him to that day's lunch: a rather more modest grape salad. 'Grapes,' he said dismissively, tutting and rolling his eyes. 'Balls of sugar'.

Earlier in her career Julie was responsible for supplying food directly to the taoiseach's office during the era of Charlie Haughey. Haughey had a higher tolerance for grapes than his eventual successor but insisted that they be hand-polished before delivery. Seemingly only the shiniest grapes were worthy of his office.

The second group without whom the place wouldn't function is the team of ushers, who fulfil every role from shepherding distinguished visitors to forming the complex's first line of external defence to acting as Leinster House's tour guides (one usher has Irish Sign Language and can deliver a signed tour for deaf visitors). Simultaneously, the ushers make for an impressive network of intelligence-gathering: little occurs throughout the Oireachtas complex without one of them picking up on it.

One usher thinks this is simply a consequence of being visible and personable. 'If we're stationed somewhere inside the building, we're here to be of service, so we make eye contact with everyone who passes by. If someone stops for a chat, they usually have some gossip.'

Ushers are in constant contact with one another to arrange the rotation of their positions and to be aware of any developing issues anywhere on the campus – so gossip can get around very quickly. Enda Kenny's abrupt announcement in 2014 of the resignation of Alan Shatter from the cabinet took all political observers and journalists by surprise – but not the ushers, who had apparently spotted the background choreography kicking into operation.

Other important players in the parliamentary landscape include committee clerks and secretariats. Most of the 'sectoral' Oireachtas committees – that is, those that oversee the work of specific government departments, and are tasked with scrutinising legislation coming from the relevant ministers – have their own full-time clerks and secretariats to organise their work. They are an important part of the functioning of the system, organising the presentations of witnesses, circulating documents and generally giving effect to the decrees of a committee.

'They're the gears that keep the whole thing in motion,' says one former committee chair. 'If you wanted, you could go into autopilot because the clerk lays everything out for you – even the legal warnings you have to give witnesses. Of course a good chair will want to be hands-on and to take a proper interest in their committee workload, but if you were only half-arsing it, the clerks would still make you look good.'

Committee clerks, this person notes, are also among the few Oireachtas staff members whose work is visible to the public. When their committee finds itself in the public eye, or with a bigger audience than usual, they might go out of their way to oversee a slick operation and impress any onlookers.

Also influential is the Office of the Parliamentary Legal Advisers (OPLA), a team of 22 lawyers and accompanying administrators who have two main roles. The primary role is to represent the legal interests of the Oireachtas against outside challenges, helping to prepare legal defences in the occasional case where the Dáil or Seanad, or their members, are sued by outsiders. Sometimes the comments of a member, or the actions of a committee, can cause ire in an interested outsider who brings the issue to the High Court. The OPLA's job is to defend these cases – and also to prevent them arising in the first place.

This can sometimes rankle with members who see the advice as overly cautious, or sometimes outright contradictory to the will of the politicians. Nonetheless the OPLA carries enormous sway. In 2022, for example, the Public Accounts Committee was presented with extraordinary evidence of what appeared to be significant financial tensions between the Department of Health and the HSE. The evidence included audio recordings of department meetings where officials suggested the HSE might be unable to account for how the vast majority of its 2020 budget – some €21 billion, swelled by the urgency of the pandemic – was actually spent. Allegations like that would ordinarily be manna from heaven for the Public Accounts Committee, but an intervention from the OPLA nipped any hearings in the bud: the people in the recordings didn't know they were being recorded, meaning the taping was illegal, and the PAC would be wandering into legally sketchy ground were its findings to be the fruit of a poisoned tree.

The OPLA's second function is to help members themselves figure out what the law is, and how to change it. This is something of an irony: TDs and senators are, by definition, lawmakers – yet unless they happen to be legally trained themselves, they often have no idea how to start translating their views into the black and white of draft legislation. The OPLA helps to bridge this divide for non-ministers, meeting with members and their assistants to thrash out clearly what the politician aspires to do and whether this is in keeping with European or other international laws, and then helps them draft legislation to make it a reality. (It can be the source of some dismay for members when, having recruited a team of in-house professionals to draft a legally sound bill, the government refuses to accept it on the premise that there are alleged flaws in its drafting.)

There's also a similarly minded offering from the Library and Research Service (LRS), which has a fairly transparent goal of ensuring a better-informed parliament. As well as managing the Oireachtas archives and making them available online so far as possible, the LRS produces digests of larger pieces of legislation at an official remove from government, allowing members to get an independent analysis of their provisions, and also produces 'spotlight' papers on areas of policy interest. One example is the rising use of data centres and their impact on the domestic electricity supply – the LRS pointed out that the supply of renewable energy to the national grid was not keeping pace with the growing demand from all sectors, and that although Ireland has become a key market for data centres worldwide, a policy decision would have to be made on whether large private users could continue to connect to the public supply.

The most commonly used tool from the LRS, however, is its range of dashboards that help TDs to get a deeper understanding of their own constituencies. The official census publications from the Central Statistics Office do include granular details on the likes of household occupancy rates, residents' nationalities and their use of public transport, but the LRS dashboards help to portray this information in a more user-friendly setting. Those members who use the dashboards say they can be an excellent way to predict issues that might come up on the doorsteps and allow them to get a head start on tackling those issues before ever starting an official canvass.

A similar specialised service is produced by the Parliamentary Budget Office, created in the wake of the financial crash of the early 2010s, and which offers independent critique of fiscal policy and public spending issues.

Perhaps the teams with the highest output are the Parliamentary Questions Office, the Journal Office and the Debates Office. The first is the single conduit for the tabling of written questions by TDs, relaying over 55,000 questions annually from members to government departments and back, vetting each question and reply for compliance with Dáil rules and data protection law. The second produces the daily 'order papers', which outline the business before the Houses. The third is responsible for producing near-verbatim transcripts, as quickly as is feasible, of every word uttered on the public record.

Staff from the Debates Office generally work on rotation every 10 minutes, and in pairs: one remains in a backroom and transcribes whatever is said by the speaker whose microphone is turned on, and who formally has the floor; another will go into the chamber itself and try to record as many off-microphone quips as may be offered. After 10 minutes, a fresh pair takes over, and the last two begin work drafting a combined transcript. Through a quirk of Dáil rules, this requires more editing than might be expected: all comments made in the Dáil and Seanad are supposed to be directed through the chair, and not directly across the floor. The transcript is retroactively amended to portray compliance with this idea: 'You don't know what you're doing,' for example, will become 'the minister does not know what he is doing.' These sanitised in-house transcripts are made available within an hour or two, and can often form the backbone of print reporting on the big exchanges of the day. That is, as long as the staff working on the transcription can figure out what's actually being said. To put it politely, some speakers are more cogent than others.

There is one other category of creature in Leinster House who enjoys a curious relationship with politicians, with each side inevitably looking for something from the other. That is the Leinster House press corps.

The Oireachtas Press Gallery enjoys a rare privilege among modern parliaments: it has delegated authority to control what journalists can or can't be admitted to the buildings. Where the majority of other parliaments have a central level of control, and can refuse admission to journalists as they see fit, the Oireachtas Press Gallery, like its Westminster counterpart, is a rare instance where the official parliamentary authorities outsource almost the entire process. When the gallery committee agrees to admit a new member, their name is simply issued to the Oireachtas staff, who issue a pass without any second-guessing. In exchange for this devolved power, the gallery operates within tight capacity constraints; there is a fixed upper limit on how many members are permitted – in other words, how many people have full-time access – with other visitors accommodated only on day passes.

Given the varied media and deadlines journalists work to, there is no uniform 'day in the life' for the press corps, but for almost everyone except the Sunday papers, the busiest day of the week is Tuesday. The day begins with a stakeout outside Government Buildings, hoping for soundbites from ministers as they arrive for the weekly cabinet meetings. By mid-morning attention turns to the paved plinth area inside the Kildare Street gates, where opposition parties will usually appear to raise concerns about some new government plan, or publicise their plans for using their own allocated slots of Dáil time that week. Tuesday afternoon marks the return of Dáil business with Leaders' Questions – the highest-profile slot of business, where the taoiseach is pressed by four opposition leaders on any number of high-profile issues. A few hours later, political correspondents are summoned to Government Buildings for briefing by the government's press secretaries on the outcomes of the cabinet meeting. Tuesday night is then often spent trying to unspin and detangle the official lines on these outcomes, hunting for pitfalls in what has been announced, or trying to tap up cabinet attendees for a steer on any conflict from inside the room. Under the constitution, the conduct of cabinet meetings is confidential, so press secretaries will only ever brief on the outcomes; it is left to enterprising journalists to seek off-the-record insider accounts of events.

Other rules are outside of the gallery's control and are enforced, with varying degrees of rigour, by the Oireachtas itself. For example, the Leinster House dress code (which notionally remains in place for all, although politicians are the supreme authority and therefore difficult to sanction for breaking it) remains in place for all media members hoping to sit in the press seating of the Dáil, Seanad and committee rooms. Men must wear a suit and tie, while women are expected to wear full business attire, and denim is expressly forbidden.

Sometimes, this has the odd consequence of journalists – especially visiting ones – being tapped on the shoulder by an usher and escorted from the chamber. In the short-term aftermath of the 2010 financial crash, one overseas journalist attended a Dáil sitting to research a report about the political temperature of a country living on EU and IMF cash. This journalist, well turned out in a new suit and shiny black brogues, took a seat on the Press Gallery within spitting distance of Luke 'Ming' Flanagan and Mick Wallace – two politicians whose adherence to a theoretical dress code was almost always zero. (One contemporary witness recalls Wallace wearing a soccer jersey, while Flanagan sported a T-shirt with the image of Oscar the Grouch from *Sesame Street*.) Unexpectedly, within a few minutes of taking his seat, the journalist was escorted back off the gallery and reprimanded because his own outfit did not include a necktie.

Ever since, a comically oversized men's suit jacket and a spare necktie hold permanent residence on the gallery's coat stand, so as to avoid any repeats.

17

SEEING AROUND CORNERS

What's so special about special advisors? 'Good question,' remarks one. 'Probably … shapeshifting? Because, when need be, you sort of become the mouth of the minister.'

The role of special advisors has existed in its current format since 1997, when the three-party government led by John Bruton sought to defuse any internal tensions by beefing up the back-room teams of coalition leaders, while also giving other cabinet members the opportunity to embrace some technocratic profes-sionalism by recruiting policy experts to act as internal counsel. A minister with private-sector experience in one field, but required by *realpolitik* to take a portfolio in another, could employ bona fide specialists to help them navigate the unfamiliar terrain.

Over time, however, the role has evolved: cabinet ministers (other than coalition leaders) are entitled to two special advisors, and routinely hire one as a specialist in media relations, with the other role retained for a policy wonk or another trusted opera-tive. The latter, more inward-facing advisor tends to come from within the minister's party ranks; one example is Kevin Dillon, who was previously the head of Fianna Fáil's policy unit and then became a special advisor to Darragh O'Brien when O'Brien was minister for housing. Matt Lynch held a similar role within Fine Gael before joining the personal staffs of Frances Fitzgerald, Si-mon Coveney, Leo Varadkar and then Simon Harris. Sometimes, over time, veteran advisors accrue on-the-job expertise: it is not uncommon for advisors to be re-recruited by further ministers because of their increasing familiarity with the nuts and bolts of party policy, and with working the levers of permanent government to get things done.

Irrespective of whether the advisor is primarily tied up in press queries or policy wonkery, their basic role is to act as a ministerial proxy. Within government circles, civil servants who cannot get hold of their line minister during a parliamentary week, given the various political and parliamentary demands on the minister's time, will approach an advisor as a go-between instead. From a press perspective, where an opposition frontbencher may have had time to answer journalists' phone calls directly, a minister is often too busy to do so, with the advisor becoming an auxiliary conduit.

This is part of the reason why so many journalists end up hopping the fence and working for ministers: rather than having any major political affinity with their new boss (though post-appointment loyalty is necessary to overcome the long hours), they are headhunted on the basis that they know 'what a journalist is looking for', and what might make the minister look good to the outside world. 'You get to a point in your career or life where you're ready for a change,' says one who made that move, 'and change comes knocking on your door ... you know, I'm at a point in my career where I've done it for X number of years, and this opportunity comes up, to do something interesting that serves the public.' Others leave jobs in media simply because of office politics, believing there is no scope for promotion; yet more have simply had their fill of journalism, with its increasing pressures, dwindling resources, shrinking headcounts and often static salaries.

The pay is certainly an attraction: the entry-level salary for a special advisor to a cabinet-level minister is just over €100,000, and many are paid around €116,000 – about the same as a TD, and significantly more than in their previous media careers. While most journalists are coy about their own personal incomes, an advisor's wage is easily tens of thousands higher than most corre-spondents in Leinster House could hope to earn.

There is often debate about whether it is healthy for democracy to have so many journalists attracted to jobs in government, with an inference that journalists tame their coverage in the hope of be-ing cherry-picked for lucrative advisor jobs in the years to follow. For whatever it's worth, the author thinks this concern is over-blown: nobody can ever predict when the next vacancy is going to arise, or whether there might be a change of government that necessitates the mass recruitment of handlers. Further, the cynical logic of producing soft coverage to secure a job is faulty; wouldn't a minister with a lucrative vacancy be more likely to offer to poach a critic and buy their silence?

That's not to say that the role of press advisors is solely to act as spin doctor. Many journalists-turned-advisors are also, in truth, simply interested by the practice of politics and curious to see life on the other side of the curtain, or whether they can bring about some kind of positive change. A few notable appointees have been plucked from the ranks of the media not to become spokespersons for ministers, but because of their significant insight into specific policy briefs that make them legitimate experts. 'If you think about it,' says one poacher-turned-gamekeeper, 'we're all publicly minded people one way or another.' The *Business Post*'s highly respected health correspondent Susan Mitchell was hired as a policy advisor by Stephen Donnelly as minister for health, while the *Irish Independent*'s environmental correspondent Paul Melia was taken on by Eoghan Murphy at a time when the Department of Housing was also responsible for climate and environmental issues.

Another influencing factor in making the switch, intertwined with that of money, is age. Where once the Oireachtas was the place newspapers sent their older and most esteemed correspon-dents, nowadays the advent of 24/7 news and the constant con-tent demands of the internet mean the beat is often covered by younger reporters who are comfortable with the multiplatform demands of the gig. This in turn means the working hours are long and often unpredictable, with more and more wrung out of reporters whose salaries remain fairly static. Consequently, those who don't see the job as a lifelong vocation will be more easily attracted to a government role: the hours may be equally long, and the job security poor, but the ability to gain influence much higher, and the pay significantly better. While taking an advisor role might forever close the door on a career in journalism, there will be no shortage of companies interested in hiring an ex-journalist who also has experience of internal government machinations. All in all, it is an understandable career leap to make – even if it may be disappointing to external purists.

An ambitious minister will often need their advisors to act as human battering rams in support of policy, figuring out and overcoming the barriers in its way. Some advisors end up becoming surrogates on pet projects, making sure that certain initiatives do not wither on the vine, maintaining pressure on civil servants who might offer passive resistance to the idea at hand. 'It's not just [liaising between] minister and press, it's minister and civil services, and being an agitator on a minister's behalf,' one says, noting that advisors are often also the contact point with others in their party, or in cabinet. A party colleague raising a concern, or advocating for a local cause, may end up going through the advisors rather than being able to sit down with the minister themselves.

Indeed, while ministers are holding the weekly cabinet meeting, the special advisors and media handlers also get together for a 'touch base' meeting in which each will give an overview of their short-term plans and sound out times of the week to schedule announcements or press conferences for maximal (or minimal) coverage. This also gives ministerial envoys a chance to pass on their concerns, first- or second-hand, about whatever is happening. 'You are the link between the political apparatus of the minister and their political colleagues. Really, you go into it making it as wide as you want,' says one.

The important aspect, almost all advisors recognise, is to always be clear that they are acting with ministerial imprimatur. It's one thing to liaise with civil servants and meet with outside bodies to further the minister's agenda as a proxy in their absence; it's quite another to start pursuing stuff which is extraneous to the central agenda. 'Civil servants don't live in some kind of void, where they're blind to the minister's actual top priorities,' says one former handler. 'Civil servants watch the news, and read the papers, and have copies of the Programme for Government, and listen to the same radio programmes as everyone else – they know what a minister genuinely wants to prioritise, and what they don't.' Advisors who act above their station and reprioritise lower-order issues that they're personally more interested in, will be quickly found out. Any successful freelance politicking eventually gets back to the desks of the minister and secretary general.

'The most precious thing that anyone in the highest level of government has is time,' says one. 'That's the reason advisors are there at all: in practical terms it's sort of like cloning the minister so that they can be represented in multiple places at the same time. A lot of the stuff on a minister's long-list [agenda] is stuff that the minister isn't too personally invested in – it's stuff that another party got added to the Programme for Government, or that civil servants had asked for, because they've spotted some procedural inconvenience that needs a legal change to get over.

'So you just can't go rogue and start pursuing stuff that the minister doesn't personally see as a big concern. If it gets done, the minister will be looking at you going, "What the fuck were you at? Why weren't you doing X or Y instead?" And then your political capital is spent, because the minister probably won't trust you, and the civil servants will always doubt whether you're following orders.'

Following orders in getting stuff done is especially important because achieving X or Y may involve taking confrontational stances against civil servants who might see the idea as misguided or having negative downstream consequences. The idealised view of a minister's writ running across a department, one ex-advisor says, is a fallacy: 'Everything is a negotiation with the civil service.' Getting major changes over the line is a battle of idealism on the part of the minister who wants the change and pragmatism on the part of civil servants who don't see the merit and think the payoff is not worth the effort. 'If they're not enthused about an idea, it won't come to your desk at all quickly ... they're doing their duty and trying to make sure a policy is evidence based. If they think something will have no effect in the real world, they won't break their backs using resources to do it. There'll be an attitude of, "Let's not kill ourselves," if they don't think a proposal is worth it.'

Isn't that fundamentally anti-democratic: isn't the very idea that the 'service' in civil service is to be in service of the minister? That depends, advisors say. If you're feeling charitable, you'll understand that civil servants are also doing what they think is best – by the terms of their employment, civil servants are officially gagged from speaking negatively about governmental policy, which is why special advisors are 'employed' by the minister rather than the department itself – and so passive obfuscation is often the closest they can get to making clear their concerns about an idea. There might also be a bit of give and take, and of reading the room: there might be small issues that officials want a minister to address quickly, but which are not politically sellable, and which might end up becoming makeweights for a bigger prize. 'The civil service can be in service of the minister, but it can feel like a negotiation rather than dictation. It shouldn't be a dictation, but nor should it be a logjam, and often it is.'

It is also worth remembering that the permanent officials standing in the way of a policy might not always be in a minister's own department. The resistance to a new social welfare idea, for example, may not be from officials in the Department of Social Protection but rather from officials on the Finance or Public Expenditure sides. In that case, a minister might need to get their counterpart to hold sway, nudging through an idea that their officials are uneasy about. Heather Humphreys was far from the first minister for social protection to pursue the idea of an auto-enrolment pensions system, so that people in the private sector might be more likely to expect a reasonable standard of living in retirement. It had never come to fruition, Humphreys says, because the officials in charge of the purse strings were concerned about an open-ended bill to the Exchequer in the event of a major economic slump. The idea finally made it onto the books in 2024 not only because of her own insistence – and a more comfortable economic climate – but because of the political backing of Michael McGrath, who made clear to his own officials, across both the Departments of Finance and Public Expenditure, that the idea carried his personal imprimatur.

Ultimately, the battle between a minister and an unwilling civil service is a test of wills, and of time, and civil servants always have an advantage on the latter. 'They're going to be there when the minister is not,' one advisor laments. 'Even if the next minister has the same priority, the clock resets at zero.'

That shortage of time is, after all, some of the reason why advisors have come to be in the first place.

Humphreys is particularly vocal about the role of special advisors in helping to shepherd through a minister's agenda in the increasingly common case where a single minister has more than one department to run. Each cabinet-grade minister can only have two advisors, irrespective of how many departments they run – which necessitated an interesting innovation when Humphreys' cabinet colleague Helen McEntee became the first cabinet minister to go on maternity leave.

The Department of Justice is an enormous ministry for anyone to take on, given the huge legislative workload it produces and the gravity of its responsibilities, from immigration to alcohol, from the courts system to gambling. During his own tenure in the job, Alan Shatter famously showed up to work seven days a week, sometimes even peppering the attorney general with work calls early on a Sunday morning. It is not a job that can be left on autopilot when a minister needs time away, as was the case twice for McEntee between 2020 and 2024.

Bunreacht na hÉireann never envisaged ministers taking maternity leave, so a constitutional novelty was concocted. McEntee would remain a full member of the cabinet – thus retaining her professional status and salary, just as any other new mother taking maternity leave would expect – but in the interim would become a minister without portfolio, while another minister would take up her duties for the six months. In the first case, that was Humphreys, who was then left running three departments at once, adding Justice to her existing roles in Social Protection and Rural and Community Development.

If her arrangements were challenging, even greater ones emerged for McEntee's two special advisors. It emerged that a minister without a portfolio was not entitled to advisors (the thinking being that a minister with no department did not need an inner team), so from the very moment she relinquished the Justice portfolio, her advisors were gone. Nor could Humphreys do without them: so much work was already in train that it was simply untenable for the special advisors to disappear as well. The solution was that the two advisors, automatically made redundant when the Justice portfolio was handed over, were immediately re-recruited by McEntee's party leader Leo Varadkar (who as tánaiste did not have the same cap on appointees), and informally seconded back to Humphreys for the duration of the role.

This offered continuity on two fronts. It ensured Justice was properly tended to, with McEntee's advisors keeping Humphreys afloat and readying her for any legislative debates in the Dáil or Seanad. It also meant the time-challenged minister had surrogates at her other two departments to keep an eye on her other priorities – and to ensure she was brought up to speed before sessions of Dáil question time, which she was still expected to handle for each of the three jobs.

'Your advisors are your eyes and ears: you have to totally trust them and believe in them. And I did that,' Humphreys says. 'The two lads [McEntee's advisors], they were very good to me. And I had my own two men looking after me in the other two departments.'

18

BEST OF ENEMIES

A long-standing TD tells a story about a time when he and a rival were booked to go on the same late-night debate programme. It is customary for political guests on late-night shows on RTÉ or Virgin Media to be offered taxis to facilitate their travel from Leinster House, or from their city-centre hotels, out to the respective studios in Montrose or Ballymount. Sitting politicians are not paid for their appearances on such programmes, so at the very least producers try to ease their transit and make it easier to secure a booking.

This particular evening, one of the two TDs had accepted the offer of a taxi; the other had declined and said they would make their own way out. The pair ended up meeting on their way out of Leinster House – one intending to take their car, the other availing of the taxi – and when they realised they were both going in the same direction, the first TD invited the second to leave their car behind and to share the taxi journey with them. In the car, the two made friendly chatter about the events of the day and their various shared pastimes.

'That night we went out and we tore strips off each other in studio,' that TD recalls. 'It was vicious, absolutely brutal. Hair flying everywhere. The sort of shouting match where the presenter has to interrupt you a few times, and tell you to take it easy, because nobody at home can hear you shouting over each other.'

After the show had gone off air, the two got back into their shared taxi, picked up their conversation where they had left off on the journey out, and shared a lift back into town together. Their respective hotel bedrooms being close to one another, they even went for a pint together before retiring for the night.

ʃ

Politics has always had an element of the pantomime. The performative bravado of candidates on the election trail, promising to be the fighting voice of the forgotten and overlooked citizens of their constituencies, inevitably translates into politicians having, as one puts it, to 'act the big fella' upon arrival. It is perhaps not too surprising that Leinster House has a reasonable population of professional wrestling fans, among both media and political practitioners. Both industries have an element of showbiz, of saying the right thing to generate heat, and of playing off the crowd to evoke the desired emotional response from the onlookers. They also have their fair share of real-life vendettas, but in the main, most protagonists are able to coexist happily behind the curtain.

Those who win a seat on the back of a vigorous and provocative campaign will be expected to keep up the same demeanour when they arrive in Leinster House. One shop window is the first sitting of the new Dáil: longer-serving TDs often pay close attention to the maiden speeches from newly appointed independent deputies, looking to see whether the newcomer strikes a constructive note or emerges all guns blazing to complain about the Dublin elites forgetting the plain people of Ireland. Rookie deputies often get more than their fair share of airtime on the first sitting of a new Dáil, especially in circumstances where a government has not yet been formed, and there may be scope for independents to join a coalition and make up the numbers in a ruling bloc. Senior figures will take mental notes on which ones could be depended upon to make a deal later.

But no more than any other human soul, politicians don't exactly respond well to attempts at public shaming. For someone who wants funding for a school extension, shouting a lot on the floor might look good to the constituents, but a request for a private meeting with the minister – or even a simple letter, making clear the urgent need for services and outlining the dismal social consequences of failing to meet it – is more likely to do the trick.

For those in opposition and on the government backbenches, trying to command a minister's attention, even on the best and most deserving of issues, is tricky. A strange sort of coalition-building emerges, where those who are ostensibly rivals can make for unlikely collaborators.

Some see this as entirely rational. 'If I'm an opposition spokesperson and I'm sitting on an Oireachtas committee, and it meets once or twice a week,' says one TD, 'and I'm seeing the spokespersons for other parties raising the same issues as me, of course it makes sense to build links and figure out how you can achieve the most together.' Notwithstanding the fracturing of the Dáil landscape, and the fact that opposition parties are just as much in competition with each other as they are with the government, there is an 'enemy's enemy' approach. Strategic collective action that weakens a government or forces a concession is to their mutual benefit. Strategic cooperation is not exclusive to opposition parties, however: there might equally be cases where government and opposition TDs align to pursue a common cause.

'Whatever our political differences, if you take the local politics, you're interested in advancing your own constituency,' says one Sinn Féin TD. 'I have a very good working relationship with the local TDs and Oireachtas members in my constituency. We have worked together on lots of issues. We will go in with one voice into lots of meetings.'

Health, and hospital services, is a topic that carries such regional importance that local TDs and senators are almost expected to rally across party lines. The shortcomings in cardiac services in Waterford, for example, unite not only Waterford TDs but those from adjoining counties whose constituents are equally endangered by inadequate service provision (it is thought that Waterford needed not only a junior minister in the Department of Health, but also persistent pressure from the opposition, to finally secure the necessary services). Persistent overcrowding in the emergency department at University Hospital Limerick equally exercises deputies from Limerick, Clare and Tipperary. A proposed downgrade of Navan Hospital was averted through near-universal local opposition.

The unity of regional TDs on local issues is sometimes taken for granted. When the Covid-19 pandemic threatened the viability of Shannon Airport, Fine Gael's Clare TD Joe Carey convened an all-party 'Shannon Airport Oireachtas Committee' – and promptly began to issue press releases describing himself as its chair, presenting himself as the face of a united front. This was news to at least one other TD in the same constituency, who had not been invited to any such committee and was more than a little perplexed to see Carey's self-awarded title being faithfully cited in the news.

One opposition TD sees this sort of cross-party unity as win-win. A single deputy might never be able to turn a constituency issue into something that commands a response from a national minister. Forming alliances with others in the area for that reason might therefore be a prerequisite, but it's also electorally useful. If the government sanctions the money for a new school building, *realpolitik* dictates that the minister is the one who claims the credit – sometimes at the expense of the government's local TD. In all likelihood, there have probably been cases where government TDs were able to grease the wheels of an application, using their greater access to make sure the minister was approached at the right moments, but opposition TDs rightly or wrongly claimed the lion's share of the credit.

In some instances, there is no need to build a coalition across the opposition benches: ministers too have a sense for good politics and might simply give an opposition counterpart a fair hearing.

One TD with experience of being an opposition frontbencher and taking the lead on Dáil question time with various ministers, has had varying experiences depending on the outlook of the minister in the opposite seat. 'Sometimes I make suggestions to make a political point and point out that the government are useless and we're brilliant, and that's part of my job,' they joke. 'But sometimes you might go quietly behind the scenes to the minister and go, "You're after pissing off stakeholder group X with this. Why are you doing this? There is no need to do it – I sort of understand what your thinking is, but you're wrong." It's genuinely a perspective that their officials haven't made them privy to before now.'

This is, however, a minority assessment. Most governments command Dáil majorities and can declare with authority that their opinion is the one with the public's approval. Most ministers – whether it is because they are stubborn, self-righteous, or beholden to their officials – have little or no appetite for truly taking opposition views on board. Gary Gannon, who found himself juggling several different responsibilities as a Social Democrats spokesperson, has been tasked with marking several different ministers and rarely found any of them willing to listen to constructive comments.

The one exception he offers is Regina Doherty – who remained as a caretaker minister for social protection during the first months of the Covid-19 pandemic, despite having lost her own seat in the Dáil. 'She was really good at ringing you up and asking what your opinions on particular things were, when it came to stuff like the three-hundred-and-fifty-euro pandemic unemployment payment. I remember myself and Regina talking about that before it was announced.' Whether that was because the pandemic was a compelling circumstance, or because Doherty had already lost an election and was liberated from straightforward party-political concerns, he couldn't tell.

One Sinn Féin frontbencher, speaking off the record, confirms they occasionally strike up strategic transactional relationships with other parties to keep up the pressure on common goals. One might put in a parliamentary question on a topic one week, share the answer with the other opposition parties, and then get them to submit a follow-up query two weeks later. It is the very antithesis of the public approach to business, where parties rarely gang up so as to better package their social media videos afterwards. The thinking is that a department, or a minister asked to approve the wording of the answer before it gets issued, will be led into thinking the matter is something of genuine cross-bench concern. When the next budget comes around, the minister might think they'll be buying a lot of goodwill or popularity by bowing to this apparently universal desire. 'They scratch your back, on a thing you want,' this frontbencher says, 'and you can scratch them back at some other stage.' Whether the ruse ever works is hard to determine, but those who participate in it find no harm in trying.

$$\Omega$$

There are some exceptions to the hands-across-the-divide rule. Paul Murphy makes a point of trying to keep a personal distance from other TDs – not so much that he's antisocial or declining to make small talk in the lift – but because becoming personally sympathetic to others outside of the socialist sphere might compromise his own politics. 'I'm very conscious of not speaking to make friends with them,' he says, 'because I think that would make your job harder – you know, maybe they [end] up being the minister and you really need to criticise them because they've done something bad, or you really need to go for them over something which may end up in them resigning … you want not to feel like, "Oh, God, this is terrible."

'I'm not saying they're bad people. Often a thing the government says is, "You think you have a monopoly on compassion." No, I don't think that – you've plenty of compassion. Simon Harris has plenty of compassion. He can go on Ryan Tubridy['s podcast about books] and show a lot of compassion for the people in Gaza, but objectively, I think he's playing a certain role in terms of Ireland's position in a world system that is dominated by the US, and that places real constraints on what he's actually doing. Despite his real compassion, which is real – he's not lying, right? – but objectively he's not doing much to help the people of Gaza.

'And on a smaller level, I'd have the same attitude in terms of John Lahart [the Fianna Fáil TD in Murphy's same constituency], or Colm Brophy [of Fine Gael] or whatever.'

On the flipside, sometimes genuine friendships blossom across parties, and indeed across generations. One Sinn Féin figure revealed an unlikely – but nonetheless close – friendship with a Fine Gael grandee, as a result of their joint membership of an Oireachtas body. Despite having very different outlooks on politics, and in particular on the future of Northern Ireland, the two became pally and now enjoy a sincere friendship. That friendship, and others they have built up outside of party confines, emerged 'from conversations around the difficulties in politics – maybe around your own personal circumstances, and then they would talk about theirs – and sometimes it's actually easier to have those conversations with people who are not in your own political party'.

'You just get on with different people. If you've friendships outside of politics, not all of them are going to vote for you,' another TD wisely observes. 'They are not all going to be political allies, you know. Some of your friends will vote for other parties, as is the case with me. So it's the same when you go into the

Oireachtas. There are people who you're just friendly with because of their personality and not their politics.'

'At the end of the day,' one senator bluntly concludes, 'your days here are too long to go around being a prick to people. You're here to get stuff done, and you get nothing done alone, and you're definitely not going to get anything done by going around and acting the bollocks all day.'

19

DEMOB HAPPY

There's a saying in politics that all careers end in failure. This is true in almost every case: it is so rare, almost unprecedented, that someone walks away at a time of their own choosing. Even those who retire on their own steam generally tend to go because of advanced age: still enthusiastic about the role, but unable to muster the physical energy to match the intellectual hunger.

Leo Varadkar was barely home from a visit to the White House in 2024 before abruptly announcing he was quitting as Fine Gael leader, and as taoiseach. The announcement stunned the political world; some of his closest aides had been told only a few days in advance. Others were told at a private reception in Washington during the trip.

The man himself, it turns out, had been harbouring doubts for a few years. 'When we formed the government in 2020 – that unusual government, which we didn't expect to happen – even then I was wondering to myself, would I, or should I, be the person to take over [when the office of taoiseach was to be rotated] in 2022.

'I did, and I gave it a go for a year, and then came to the conclusion that on the political side, I didn't have the political capital to be the right person to lead the party into the next election. But also, in my own head, I didn't love it so much that I was devastated to leave.'

Heather Humphreys' departure was only slightly less of a surprise when she announced seven months later that she would not contest the general election around the corner. When Varadkar resigned she had been touted as a prospective party leader; she and Simon Harris reached an accommodation (of undisclosed compromise) where she would allow him to go unchallenged and take the role of deputy leader instead. There had been suggestions she might be eyeing up a run for president. Someone who had always been perceived as energetic – and who was broadly liked around Leinster House, by those from other parties as well as her own – was suddenly leaving. At 64, she might have expected to have had another term in her.

'After the locals,' she says, referring to the local elections of 2024, 'I just … I was tired. To be honest with you, I'm at this quite a while now, and working a long time. I thought I'd get the energy up again, but it just didn't come. And I said, "Here, this is the time." I'm around long enough to know it's time to move off the pitch. There's nothing seriously wrong with me or anything – I just don't have the same level of energy as I used to.'

Being a deputy leader of her party meant, in the event of Fine Gael returning to government, there would have been an expectation of returning to cabinet and facing into another few years of the treadmill of juggling constituency work, a busy ministerial diary and the extra duties that come attached to a party leadership position. It was, in short, not a workload she could commit to keeping up. Many of her friends and contemporaries at home were reaching retirement age, and seeing them prepare for a comfortable life had its draws.

There was one other factor. 'You start to run out of ideas,' says Humphreys. Serving in five different departments over 10 years left her without any new projects to pursue.

ʒ

For others, there is no shortage of ideas: many are continually sustained by the intellectual challenge of the national arena. Richard

Bruton was also getting ready for retirement when interviewed for this book, aged 71, at the end of a 43-year parliamentary career entailing 11 successive general election wins from February 1982. Fianna Fáil's Willie O'Dea entered the Dáil at that same election – serving long enough to qualify for the full parliamentary pension twice over – but had not yet had his fill of public life, and was running again in the 2024 election. So too was Bernard Durkan, at the age of 79, having first become a TD in June 1981.

'I love every dimension of the job,' Bruton said, unapologetically. 'I love the constituency work – I canvassed twice a week for forty-three years, I enjoy that. I like that rapport with the people. And I suppose,' he adds with a self-effacing touch, 'like all politicians, I like the sound of my own voice.'

Even after 43 years in Leinster House – eight months in the Seanad and 42 years in the Dáil – and after 11 years in cabinet with four different ministries, he found the notion of public recognition still had its attractions. 'I like to see some recognition of the work I'm doing being reported, or getting a chance to argue your case in the media. I've never lost that interest. What has sustained me also, even at times when I'm not in ministries – I still have considerable leverage in policy terms around issues, and so I've been able to position myself as an economist and a research-type person, and can continue to influence thinking from outside.'

Researching and contributing to policy is one thing, but implementing it is its own joy. Mary Harney once quipped that someone's worst day in government was always, invariably, better than their best day in opposition. Bruton agreed. 'A day in ministry is worth an awful lot of time on the opposition benches … but I still enjoy the game.

'I think I probably would go another forty years,' he said, as his own retirement came into view in late 2024. 'I will miss it.'

꠸

Bruton, Varadkar and Humphreys were among 17 Fine Gael TDs elected in 2020 who decided not to contest the election at the end of 2024 and to do something else with their lives. The new Dáil was expanding, gaining 14 seats, and many of those TDs might have been able to comfortably hold their seats if so minded. The mass exodus raised some questions for Fine Gael, given how many departures came from that party, but also about the nature of modern-day politics as a whole.

There is no single reason behind their various retirements, but interviews with many underlined a few mutual themes. Firstly, there was age: Fine Gael had gained so many seats in 2011, arising from Fianna Fáil's electoral collapse, that there was a generation of TDs aged 60 or more whose careers had reached a natural end. Then there were figures who had served as ministers from 2016 to 2020, in an era when Fine Gael's minority government had more ministers than backbenchers, and who lost their ministries in 2020 when their party found itself sharing power with two others. For many, getting a ministerial role, and then having to give it up again, was a sign of a career that had already peaked. (One notes that the Balkanisation of the Dáil, and the decline of large parties into medium-sized blocs, means a higher expectation of a ministry earlier in a TD's career.)

Thirdly, however, was the idea that full-time politics is a tougher game now than it used to be. 'Maybe it's a generational thing – the idea that millennials don't commit their entire lives to one career,' says one relatively young retiree. But, from this slightly younger figure's perspective, the pace of the job and the variety of publicity demands make the role a little bit too challenging to sustain long term. 'It just feels', they say, 'like there's more on our plates now than there ever used to be before.'

The obligations of social media, and the perception of politicians being as 'always on' as the news cycle, are widely cited as reasons why so many get out so quickly.

'It's at the point now where you can't even bring your kids to the cinema for two hours, and keep your eyes off the phone,' one opines. 'You're expected to be always on. It's not just the risk of a constituent getting upset if you don't pick up when they ring – it's the presumption that you're obliged to make some kind of public statement if some major global tragedy happens. If you don't do it within half an hour, people will say you're heartless. No, lads, I do genuinely care – it's just that I've brought the kids to see *Despicable Me 4* and I'm not looking at my phone.'

Another thinks the cynicism directed at politicians isn't exclusive to them – and that the nature of society is that ordinary people are more assertive in the face of a challenge from someone else in a position of influence. 'You have teachers getting attacked by parents now, you know? When I was in school, if I got in trouble with teacher, I'd be in trouble with my mam. Nowadays, Mam will go down to the teacher and probably have a row with them.'

TDs of longer standing acknowledge their fortune in getting in the game, and being able to build up a political profile, without having needed to play the game of online engagement. 'I find it terribly depressing,' says one such older figure. 'It's burning an awful lot of people out. I never allowed it to depress me the way I see some colleagues getting deflated by it. I just plough on, counting my blessings that I've built enough of a constituency profile that I don't need to.'

Richard Bruton is forthright about the role that instantaneous hot takes can play in the public space. 'It's so corrosive … we will destroy deliberative politics of the sort that I would value: to take time to reach conclusions about what needs to be done, and you listen – if you have to have your answer right, on day one, before you've given it any thought …'

The cynicism of it wears other people down. An almost universal refrain among TDs and senators is that, where once social media was a chance to cut through the noise and communicate directly with voters in a way that was both personable and respectful, it has now become so permanently hostile that it no longer allows for two-way engagement, thus defeating the point. 'You're always one message away', says Labour's Duncan Smith, 'from feeling like you've dropped the ball on something – and that that message can come right in the middle of a Wednesday afternoon, or it can come in a Facebook message at seven o'clock on a Sunday morning.'

ȣ

For Brendan Griffin, the change of pace during the Covid-19 pandemic was an illustration of how life could simply take other paths. After he had spent three years as a junior minister for tourism and sport – including four months as a caretaker minister, trying to salvage some of the sectors worst hit by the pandemic – the formation of a new coalition government in June 2020 meant fewer ministries for Fine Gael and a relative demotion to the non-ministerial role of party whip. After three years of intensive travel and overnight absences, work life suddenly reconcentrated around Leinster House, the Convention Centre where the Dáil was holding its socially distanced sittings, and work in his constituency.

He gave his interview for this book over the phone, during a Dáil recess in what he knew would be his final term. That morning, he said, 'I had the lads got up for school, and got them off, and I'll be [there] this afternoon when they come home; tomorrow one of them has a soccer match, and I'll be there with him, and there's other stuff coming up at the weekend. I know, for a fact, I couldn't do any of that if I was a minister.'

ȣ

One surprisingly common view espoused by politicians is that they sometimes feel trapped by their own careers: when it takes such hard work to climb the pole, and to make it into Leinster House and perhaps into Government Buildings, it feels like a defeat or a betrayal, or both, to simply lay down the arms and walk away.

'I can definitely think of at least half a dozen TDs who would walk away in the morning, if they didn't feel like they would be letting down the people who got them in in the first place,' says one politician who walked away from a career that still had the potential of further advancement.

Why? If the job is so fulfilling, why feel trapped? Firstly, because the professional cost–benefit relationship may be unreasonable: delivering for constituents might be one thing, but if there is little scope of getting towards cabinet to make a more meaningful difference, then it is professionally a dead end, running to stand still – and secondly, because the opportunity cost is not worth it. The grind, the slog, the mileage, the early starts, the late nights, the working weekends, the time away from home … is it worth it for a precarious job with a higher-than-average share of abuse? A growing number are of the mind to simply do other things; retreat, be grateful for the opportunity, and reorient their lives for the remainder.

Yet there is a resistance – partly because the job they hold may be the most important they'll ever have, and partly because getting elected is such a team effort. 'So many people work so hard to get you where you are that you feel like it would be an insult to them to simply throw your hat at it,' says one. Another cites the team nature of politicians' offices: a decision to retire also means putting parliamentary and administrative assistants, and ministerial special advisors, out of work.

One politician is of the view that many TDs feel elections should be closer together: a five-year term is too long. They suggest that committing to the principle of being a TD for five years requires too much medium-term change to someone's personal circumstances and those of their family. Their perception is that if the guaranteed lifetime of the Dáil were shorter – say, with fixed terms of three years, as is done in New Zealand – then politicians might be more likely to make a commitment knowing the change in their circumstances might not be forever. You might tolerate missing kids' school plays or sports matches for a couple of years, and your partner might understand that one or two anniversaries might have to go on the back burner. But it's not forever. A five-year commitment means having to move so much of the furniture of life that members become institutionalised almost by necessity. So much sacrifice has been made – the early starts, the late finishes, the nights away, the missing weekends – that the old life is barely recognisable, even barely salvageable.

A term of three or four years, this politician thinks, would give more people scope to consider running at least once, and leave open the option of having a meaningful life to walk back to if one decides not to run a second time. As it is, they argue, the five years become so much of a slog that the sacrifice must be vindicated by running again. It is an idea they declined to put their name to, but hoped might garner some currency.

Epilogue
IS THAT ALL THERE IS?

This book is supposed to be about politicians and the lives they lead, and not about its author, but I hope you'll forgive a small personal anecdote for the sake of illustration.

For five years I juggled my day job as a political correspondent with Virgin Media News with a side role as a radio presenter, hosting a two-hour Sunday mid-morning news magazine show on Newstalk. That full-time period, from spring 2019 to autumn 2023, had been a time of huge change for Ireland and the world, with a general election and a global pandemic, and I'd found the job stimulating and rewarding. Trying to help people navigate the tumult of Covid-19, and find some clarity in the maelstrom, was always worth getting out of bed for, even in the darkness of a chilly winter Sunday morning.

Those five years had been a time of huge change for me too: my wife and I had welcomed two daughters into the world, in July 2019 and September 2021. By summer 2023, the younger child – born on a Sunday evening, with the earliest stages of labour kicking off while I was in the radio studio – was beginning to notice her daddy's absence for the first half of every Sunday. Daddy, too, was beginning to appreciate that it wasn't just his own Sunday mornings (and Saturday nights) he was giving up: Mammy's weekend was also indefinitely compromised by holding the fort while Daddy was gone. The show had been rewarding and enjoyable to do, but the personal consequences had begun to weigh on me too heavily: in summer 2023 I handed in my notice, and finished the show that September, only announcing my departure in the last five minutes of my final programme. It wasn't as if I was staring into some kind of professional or financial abyss: I still had my day job at Virgin Media News.

Two days later I was doing some filming outside the gates of Government Buildings when a senior TD came walking towards me. This deputy was not someone I'd consider to be especially close: we would always exchange passing salutations on corridors, but had never chatted about anything either of us would consider personal. Yet the TD bounded up to me excitedly: 'You're giving up the radio!' I am, yes, I explained: I'd been doing it five years, my daughters are four and two now, and they're beginning to notice me being gone so much.

Quickly, there was a small but definitive change in the TD's demeanour. You're doing the right thing, they said: nothing replaces being around for your kids, and nothing can make up for the moments you miss. 'Mine are fairly grown up now, but sometimes if they're annoyed they'll look at you and tell you, "There might as well have been no daddy in this house sometimes,"' he said, his bottom lip betraying a quiver. He turned and walked on, as if wounded by his own memory.

This is not unusual when speaking to politicians. One bubbling undercurrent among members is the amount of family time sacrificed in the pursuit of political office. One member with young children mentions small talk with older colleagues, telling them what class their kids were now entering in school, 'and they'd mention their grown-up son in Chicago, or their daughter in San Francisco, and the mentions are always tinged with regret, if not outright soaked with it.'

So acute is the pressure that one male politician admitted, in the course of this book, that he had been so distant through his youngest child's early life that he had no firsthand memories of their toddler years. Were it not for a healthy stock of photographs taken in his absence, the parent would be entirely unable to imagine how his youngest child had looked at that age.

𝄢

Do some in Leinster House suffer from Stockholm syndrome, becoming beholden to and even supportive of the stifling working conditions? In interviews for this book, the question seemed to catch one TD by surprise, and caused them to dwell.

It depends, it turns out, on how long the politician stays in the mindset of job-as-privilege and can avoid thinking of it as job-as-slog. For as long as politicians know little different, and simply accept the long hours and public criticism as an occupational necessity, it seems they become blinkered regarding how routine and structured a 'normal' job can be.

The Covid-19 pandemic was an enormous turning point: a reality check for some who had normalised the idea of leaving home at 8 a.m. on a Tuesday morning, not being back until Thursday evening, then missing all of Friday, Saturday and half of Sunday for constituency clinics and obligatory appearances at local events. Lockdown certainly constrained the ability of TDs to do fundamental elements of the job – constituency clinics were abandoned; personal cases became much harder to pursue when civil servants were all scrambling to find a work-from-home solution that could actually work; Dáil business was largely put on ice as the government figured out the nuances of how parliamentary privilege would work in a virtual environment – but highlighted the rhythms of home and family life that they had grown unused to enjoying.

The ability of politicians to stay the course, and to make politics a full-time career for life, might well depend on the reasons they got involved in the first place. Some politicians, it seems, are sustained by politics as a science: the policy formation, the argument, the implementation, the executive action, the unexpected consequences, the remedy, the workaround, the enactment. The *doing*. For them, securing a job in government is the North Star of achievement, the overriding motivation for going to work and dealing with all the other consequences of the job. Sometimes the compulsion to contribute is so strong that it outlives a term in government: some careers have unlikely second acts because a politician refuses to be superseded by younger colleagues and remains vocal and enthusiastic.

Others are compelled less by the pursuit of power and more by the duty of being a parliamentarian. They run for election not with the aspiration of getting a ministry, but with the noble goal of simply serving constituents. That's probably why 79-year-old Bernard Durkan of Kildare North chose to run again in 2024: just as remarkable as his 42-year continuous term in the Dáil is the fact he had only once held a junior ministerial title, and then for only 30 months. Such was Durkan's age that, during the peak of the Covid-19 pandemic, he was one of the few TDs who was supposed to observe public health advice by 'cocooning'. He didn't: instead, he continued to show up for Dáil debates and votes, and remained one of the most prodigious users of the parliamentary question system. Durkan would lodge queries about anything from the adequacy of school places and staffing to the further development of the EU's single market to the maintenance of local transport services and amenities to the vulnerability of foreign direct investment – all on a single day (those are some of the questions he lodged on 11 July 2024).

Some colleagues privately drew comparison with Brooks, a character from *The Shawshank Redemption*, who struggles with life outside of the prison he had made his home. Better to maintain the pace of life as a TD than to slow down and invite the fatigue to catch up.

Nonetheless, everyone's moment in the sun ends eventually. Durkan was defeated in November 2024, in his twelfth general election. His own appetite had never waned, but the electorate had moved on.

ℛ

Marc MacSharry left the Dáil with no regrets about his fractured relationship with Fianna Fáil, yet annoyed about what he saw as the increasing irrelevance of TDs themselves. 'The last good government in this country was from 1997 to 2002,' he contends. 'Bertie [Ahern] had eighteen months as leader beforehand; he engaged the entire party in going off in a hundred different directions to put together thirty policy documents that were founded on real people's opinion. They came in; for good or for bad they implemented that plan; and then in 2002 the plan changed.'

That second government saw a mushrooming sector of arm's-length regulators and executives, ostensibly removing many fields from the interference of politicians, with the consequence of diluting accountability from politicians too. Instead of serving the public, MacSharry believes, the purpose of government changed 'and became, "How do you stay in government forever?" And then it became about "How the fuck can we get rid of Health?"' The creation of the HSE as an arm's-length management vehicle should have been a victory of efficiency, but helped to create an ongoing pattern where ministerial decisions are increasingly paused pending the input of an outside advisory body.

This 'corporate consultancy complex', as he sees it, means the government ultimately governs less – which may be convenient for those at the cabinet table, but makes the substance of a backbencher's job all the harder. 'This generation of politicians are totally risk averse,' MacSharry believes, with the subcontracting of decisions ultimately meaning the subcontracting of accountability too.

Throw in the overzealous use of the party whip to enforce the government's view, reducing elected lawmakers to the status of lobby fodder, and MacSharry believes there is a case for simply deciding to turn one's back on parliamentary life.

Eoghan Murphy has a complementary criticism of how politics now works. Before the high-profile challenges of his time as a cabinet minister, and his eventual dramatic departure from politics, he had been vocal about the perception of backbench TDs as parliamentary automatons who were often unable to exert any influence of their own.

'You want to have a system whereby individual backbenchers can champion legislation, or certain changes to legislation,' he says, 'whereby there's enough potential reward for them in being able to do things. The structure, as it is, is built way too much towards trying to get into office, as if that's the most important thing. If you're a complete outsider, you might never go into office, and so you're [left] trying to get your fifteen-second TikTok clip from the Dáil of you saying something really outrageous against the minister. It doesn't lend itself to people who might want more of a middle-of-the-road career and to just be a good legislator.'

The seeming lack of an incentive for people to remain engaged in professional politics, other than to pursue ministerial office, is for him a structural flaw of the Irish system. 'When you look at other political structures in other countries, being a good legislator is everything. Being a good senator in America is everything – it can be as important as being a governor of a state in many people's lives, even more important than being the vice-president. Yet in the Irish system, being simply a legislator … it's something, but it's not what it could be.'

Murphy's take has echoes in the outlook of Gary Gannon. 'I'm quite honest with constituents: I felt like I'd more power or influence as a city councillor than I do as an opposition TD, which is why it's not how I want to spend the majority of my time in politics.'

It's a blunt, and striking, critique of life as a national parliamentarian, but it's one he sticks to. 'I can't imagine why anybody would want to do opposition politics for too long.

'The time where I was most able to get things done was that brief period I had when I was elected to [Dublin] City Council for a second time. You'd have nothing at the moment which is comparable to that. Even if you write a parliamentary question, the answers are generally formulated in a way that – even if they were to change their mind – you certainly wouldn't be getting any credit for it.'

And yet people keep choosing to run, even knowing the pitfalls, even knowing the general powerlessness, knowing the ability to make an impact is far lower than outsiders may think.

Noel Rock didn't get to leave on his own terms the first time around. Dublin North-West was always a marginal seat at best for Fine Gael, a solidly working-class constituency where a candidate for a centrist and sometimes cerebral party like Fine Gael – even if themselves from firm working-class roots – would struggle. After he scraped to victory in 2016, a post-census boundary review cut off a large chunk of his voters and transferred them to Dublin Central. The cloud had a silver lining for the party, with hundreds of more reliable Fine Gael votes transferring to Dublin Central and buffering the position of Paschal Donohoe. That was scant consolation for Rock, whose own personal share of the vote rose in what was left of his constituency, but who could not fight the national tide in 2020. Fianna Fáil took his seat.

He offers a more tangible example of the gratification that keeps politicians coming back. 'I went to a small flower shop after filming my candidate video,' he said, in the midst of a late and last-minute return to politics to contest the 2024 election.

'I wanted to pick up some flowers for [his partner] Dawn, as I know life is tough, and I know being the partner of a candidate is tougher again. There's a lot of mud these days, and it's hurtful for family and loved ones to see that.

'Anyway, I pick up some nice flowers, and the owner recognises me, and asks if it is indeed me. She tells me we've never met, but that she emailed me a decade ago to help with an issue regarding her son. She says I got back to her, [that I] was incredibly helpful, that she got what she needed, and her son was doing well a decade on. I was delighted, and even as I retell it, I still am.

'Governments and departments are labyrinthine. We can help citizens to navigate them, and where we find flaws when helping citizens navigate them, we can actually go and work to fix those flaws. What a great privilege.'

That, ultimately, was the reason he went back. Having lost his seat in 2020 he set up – and then sold – a consultancy business specialising in the overlap between technology and public affairs. But many who lose their seats, and do well in other lines of work, still feel the pull. There is (almost) always an appetite to go back and do more, to give it another go, to take one more spin on the proverbial merry-go-round. Rock's return did not work out in his favour, with him coming fifth in a three-seat constituency, but in his own mind it was better to have one more try than to forever wonder if things could have ended differently.

Another ex-TD admits to struggling with the label of 'former' politician. 'You're forever a politician,' they say, with a candid level of introspection. 'No matter what else you do in your life, you know you've already written the first line of your obituary. "Mr X was a member of Dáil Éireann for however many years." If that's how you're going to be remembered, you want to make your mark.'

It's a surprisingly universal sentiment around members' offices. One former government backbencher had the letters O-H-I-O cut out of giant pieces of paper and tacked to the wall of her office. What's that about? her colleagues asked. Are you some kind of U.S. election maniac, obsessing about a crucial swing state? No, came the eventual reply; it's an acronym. Only Hold It Once. Don't expect to get a second chance at this job; make your one chance count.

Duncan Smith feels the same way. Undeterred by a term in opposition, or the long odds of ever holding a ministerial job, he wants to hang tough. 'It's a very special job, and you have an opportunity for that period you're in there to help and to make a difference. And you can do that with individuals, which is very rewarding, but you also have an opportunity to move the conversation on big, national, important issues, and to actually amend legislation, and to start conversations in areas where there isn't a conversation going. I'm not saying I've achieved any or all of those things, but that is what keeps you going: trying to do that.

'I read an interview with one of the soap stars, where he said some actors feel sorry for him because he's only ever known for that role, you know? And he said he thought it was such a great privilege to be associated with it. I feel a kind of similar thing: this is an important, special job, and I'd love to keep doing it, and I'd love to get to be a minister at some stage, and experience other elements of this job and progress with it.

'But if I don't, I'm very privileged to have done what I've done. Whatever way the road goes, I'm prepared for it.

'If I turn up at a count centre and shake hands and walk out after falling short at election time … then of course in the short term, I'll worry about my next job. But notwithstanding, I'll be okay. I know that there's a life beyond this, and there's a lot of positives to that, but this is the privilege for as long as it lasts. I think that's a good outlook to have.'

ꞁ

For those leaving the game – and those togging out for another term – hope springs eternal. There is always some new cause that energises people and pulls them into the political arena. The referendums on marriage equality, and on access to abortion, were big ones. Becoming active in the 2018 abortion referendum lit the spark in Holly Cairns. The following year she won a seat on the county council by a single vote, by 2020 she was a member of Dáil Éireann, and by 2023 she was a party leader. The ascent simply might never have happened had the referendum not been called.

In one sense, some politicians believe that being public about the challenges they face, and the visibility of the criticism they receive online, makes the working conditions oddly transparent. Future candidates will be in little doubt about the sort of life they might face, and this might perversely embolden somebody who would otherwise back down for fear of the unknown. Entering the area with eyes wide open might disabuse some of any delusions of politics having an overall genteel tone – but means that others can psych themselves up for the job long before filing the paperwork to run.

Regulars at The Sheds bar in Clontarf were a little amused when their young barman Barry Heneghan told them he was thinking of running for the city council. Heneghan, 25, had been an active community volunteer fundraising for mental health charities, but had never expressed any real interest in electoral politics. Moreover, it was March when he started telling customers about his plans; most thought he'd left it a bit late to start knocking on doors as a newcomer.

What Heneghan lacked in experience, he made up for in sincerity and enthusiasm. Not only could he empathise with the challenges of housing affordability – working as a civil engineer on county council projects in the southside, while still living with his parents in Clontarf on the northside – but he could also point to inequalities in services on both sides of the city. 'I saw firsthand how much investment and attention went into certain areas compared to north Dublin, and I thought, "This is bollocks – someone needs to step up and start highlighting the lack of local amenities in north Dublin."' A particular point of contention was the delay in building Clontarf's flood defences, with unsightly yellow sandbags dumped along the shore for years as an interim measure.

'I was sick of broken promises affecting my generation, and I wanted to take accountability and throw my name in the hat,' he says. 'There's no point just complaining – go out and run, and put your name out there.'

After a three-week campaign, he won a seat on Dublin City Council in June 2024, assisted by the mentorship of former TD Finian McGrath, and brought that momentum into a general election five months later. Despite only polling in eighth place on first preferences, he took the fourth seat in Dublin Bay North.

It was a baptism of fire. The outcome of that election meant Fianna Fáil and Fine Gael needed the backing of others to form a government, and Heneghan found himself as part of a negotiating bloc with other independent TDs to provide the crucial support. Some of Heneghan's supporters were dismayed at the idea of their new TD backing a government of establishment parties and used social media to make their positions known. Heneghan, at least, went into the job knowing how hostile the internet could sometimes be. 'I do see all the abuse online, but no matter what I do, there's going to be people who don't like it. But listen, that's it: online is just noise, it's cheap shots, and that comes with the job … working is where the real work gets done. It doesn't happen in comments sections.

'The thing is, I didn't get involved in this to be adored by everyone: I got involved in this to make a change.'

ʅ

What most politicians appear to want, it seems, is for people to give politicians – and politics itself – a fair hearing. 'I was here one day in my office,' says Heather Humphreys, 'and I said, "Oh, what am I going to do?" "Well, you have two choices," one of the officials says to me. He's very good. "You're in a room. There's two doors. If you open one door, it's a raging fire, and if you open the other door, it's hungry lions."'

Any politician ever entrusted with a meaningful level of authority or executive power is faced with making decisions that are never as black-or-white as they may appear from the outside. Narratives can change, Humphreys accepts, and ministers are often perceived not merely as public representatives but also as bean-counters happy with causing misery if the fiscal situation demands it.

'Most people are reasonable, but they probably don't understand that a problem that sounds simple to solve isn't quite as easy as it appears. Somebody once said, "If I solve that one, I'll create five more." Politics is such that you have to look at it in the round and see if there's unintended consequences – so I might meet somebody on the street, and they'd say, "Well, I don't know why you're not doing this, because this would be a great idea." And I'd say, "Well, now that sounds easy, but it wouldn't just be as easy as it might appear, because if I did this, that might happen, and what happens?" and this and that. When you start to give them some of the options, then they start to understand it's never black and white.

'Politicians are human, and we all go in to do our best,' she concludes. 'When I got elected first, it was to try and make a difference – to listen to the people and to be their voice, because that's what you are, first and foremost, when you get elected. You are the voice of the people who sent you, and it's up to you to hear them and try and talk to them as much as you can.'

Being elected by fellow citizens and being sent to Leinster House with the power to make rules for the rest of the country is an extraordinary privilege. Even lifelong public representatives never tire of the honour and are often overwhelmed with emotion on the day of an election count as their work is validated by the electorate and a fresh term handed over.

Having spent over 10 years on the beat at Leinster House, I have come to understand that many politicians take this privilege so seriously that they are wary of speaking too openly about the challenges of the job. By their nature, politicians have good antennae for how the public feels; public representatives on a €116,000 salary aren't likely to receive a very generous hearing when they put their heads above the parapet to vent about the secret life of Leinster House.

But while mandates from fellow citizens are sacred, those who receive them are not. To err is human, and Leinster House is a workplace where practitioners must navigate not only the glare of public attention, but also an especially intense variety of office politics.

'I wish', says one, 'it wasn't such a pantomime to get stuff done. But it is. You might as well put the chin up and get on with it.'

Glossary

Backbenchers

Members of a party – especially a party in government – who are not ministers or spokespersons. By comparison, those who hold a ministerial role, or are an opposition spokesperson on a specific area, are called **frontbenchers**. As the name suggests, frontbenchers will sit at the front of their party's seating area in the Dáil chamber, while backbenchers sit further behind.

By-election

An election to fill a vacant seat in the Dáil or Seanad in the course of its term, outside of a full general election.

Cabinet

The group formed by the taoiseach, tánaiste and 13 other senior ministers who collectively make up the government. On the day of their own appointment, the taoiseach will announce their nominees to fill the other cabinet positions. Sometimes the words 'cabinet' and 'government' are used interchangeably; the word 'government' is the official name of the cabinet – its members are 'members of the government' – but the word 'government' can also be used to refer to the entire membership of the parties in a coalition, including backbenchers.

Ceann Comhairle

The Dáil's chairperson, chosen by members to oversee the daily running of business in the chamber. The title literally translates from Irish as 'head of the council'. The equivalent role in the Seanad or in Oireachtas committees is the 'Cathaoirleach', literally meaning 'person in the chair'.

Chief Whip

The whip of the main party in government, who is largely responsible for ensuring the government's agenda is pushed through the Dáil, both by managing its timetable and ensuring that the government's TDs vote as expected.

Committees

Groups of TDs and senators that are formed to focus on more specific and specialised areas of Oireachtas business. These committees are responsible for considering proposed new laws on a detailed line-by-line basis (called 'committee stage of a bill') and holding hearings with interest groups and relevant bodies.

Deputy

A member of the Dáil, also known as a TD (Teachta Dála). When in the chamber, non-ministers are usually referred as 'Deputy', for example, 'Deputy Murphy'.

Dáil Éireann

The lower house of the Oireachtas, comprised (at the time of writing) of 174 TDs. Commonly known simply as the 'Dáil', an Irish word meaning 'congress' or 'assembly'.

Division

The technical name for a vote in either the Dáil or Seanad. The Ceann Comhairle will say that, for example, 'a division has been challenged', and the transcript of proceedings will say 'the Dáil divided' before listing the result. The name derives from the time before electronic votes, where debates were settled by members walking up a central staircase and then dividing into two directions, walking through one lobby if they were in favour and the other if they were opposed. This method of taking votes is still sometimes used in the Seanad but is no longer used in the Dáil.

Frontbenchers
see *Backbenchers*.

General election
The nationwide election held when the previous Dáil has been dissolved or reached the end of its natural life, where adult citizens vote to choose the members of the next Dáil.

Junior Minister
See *Minister of State*.

Leaders' Questions
The time during a Dáil sitting when leaders of opposition parties can put questions to the taoiseach on a matter they consider important. This is often the highest-profile slot of any sitting day in the Dáil.

Member
A Member of either House of the Oireachtas, i.e. a TD or a senator.

Minister
A member of the Government who is responsible for the policy of a department.

Minister of State
A member appointed by the taoiseach to assist a minister in the running of a government department. Often referred to more casually as a 'junior minister' (the two terms are used interchangeably). Ministers of state are intended to take political responsibility for a specific area and will sometimes have legal powers transferred to them so that they can make executive decisions on behalf of the government. Almost all of them are TDs, but some have come from the Seanad.

Motion
A proposal made in the Dáil or Seanad, which may be debated and voted on by the members.

Oireachtas
The overall name for the parliament of Ireland, which is made up of the President, Dáil Éireann and Seanad Éireann. In general, any new law requires the approval of all three components of the Oireachtas before it can be approved and take effect. The Dáil and Seanad are collectively known as the 'Houses of the Oireachtas'.

Pairing
An agreement where, if one member of the Dáil or Seanad cannot be present for a vote, a member from the opposing side agrees not to vote, thus allowing both members to be elsewhere. The principle behind pairing is that a member who is absent on official business – such as a minister on an overseas trip or someone who is on medical leave – should not have to hurry back for every individual vote. Pairing arrangements are usually organised by the party whips.

Parliamentary Question (PQ)
A question put by a TD to a minister. A small number ('priority questions') are singled out to be answered in the chamber; others will be answered in person if time allows, but the vast majority receive written replies which are published as part of the Dáil transcript.

Private Members' Business
The time allotted to opposition parties and groupings, during which they can bring forward their own proposed motions and legislation for debate. Legislation tabled by non-ministers are referred to as 'private members' bills'. There are usually two slots of private members' business each week.

Programme for Government

The document published by a new government when it begins its term, outlining its plans for its time in office. It is the product of negotiations that take place between various parties following a general election. A draft version is usually published first, so that the members of a party can vote on whether their party should participate in any proposed coalition.

Referendum

A vote by the general public on a possible amendment to the constitution.

Seanad Éireann

The 'upper house' of the Irish parliament, sometimes known as the 'Senate'. Members of the Seanad are often referred to as senators but sometimes by the comparable Irish word, *seanadóirí*. With the exception of certain legislation dealing with money, all legislation must be approved by both the Dáil and Seanad before they are sent to the President to be signed and become law.

Secretary General

The highest-ranking civil servant in any specific government department, who is responsible for the day-to-day management and governance of that department.

Sitting day

An individual day on which the Dáil or Seanad sits and conducts business. There are typically about 120 sitting days each year, usually a Tuesday, Wednesday or Thursday. By comparison, a 'session' means a term of sittings. For example, the 'spring session' of the Dáil will include a few dozen individual sittings between January and Easter.

Standing Orders

The internal rules of the Dáil and Seanad under which the two houses conduct their business.

Tánaiste

The taoiseach's deputy. In coalition governments it is common for the taoiseach to be the leader of one party and the tánaiste to be the leader of another.

Taoiseach

The head of the Irish Government. Often referred to abroad as the prime minister of Ireland.

Teachta Dála (TD)

A member of the Dáil; the Irish equivalent of the title of 'MP' used in other English-speaking countries. It translates directly from Irish as 'deputy to the Dáil'. TDs will commonly have those letters printed after their name when it appears in writing, e.g. Seán Murphy TD.

Topical Issue

An issue of concern that a TD raises in the Dáil and to which a minister responds; time is allocated on each Dáil sitting day to take up to four Topical Issues

Whip

A member appointed by each party to ensure the party as a whole is best represented by assigning speaking time and encouraging party members to vote in the desired way. Members who do not vote as desired are said to 'lose the whip' and are often suspended from their party as punishment.

Acknowledgements

It goes without saying that there simply wouldn't be a book here at all without the generosity and openness of the TDs, senators, political staff, special advisors, officials and others around Leinster House who were willing to share their insights about the ups and downs of their professional lives. I am indebted to those who told their stories, whether on or off the record, for helping me to piece together what I hope is a faithful picture of what it's like to operate at the top level in Irish politics.

What might be less apparent is that I owe the existence of this book to Aisling, as in, *Oh My God, What A Complete Aisling*. It was her creators Emer McLysaght and Sarah Breen who passed on my contact details when Gill were sounding out prospective authors for future releases. So thanks to you, Aisling, and your magnificent makers.

Gill have been a dream to work with from the very off – from the first meeting on a rainy Friday afternoon in Terenure, to the finished article. I am enormously grateful to Teresa Daly for taking the punt on publishing me; Margaret Farrelly and Esther Ní Dhonnacha for their editing and counter editing; Deborah Marsh for handling the legalities, Charlie Lawlor for her work on marketing; and Fiona Murphy and Mia O'Reilly for handling publicity.

Particular thanks to Graham Thew for his spectacular cover artwork.

If ever there were moments when I was a bit of a grump from trying to juggle the extra workload of churning out a book alongside a day job and a podcast, Richard Chambers and Zara King never let it show. Thanks, pals.

Thanks too to Ruairí Carroll at Virgin Media News, who has supported this project from the first moment I broached it with him.

My colleagues in the Leinster House press corps, past and present, are endlessly informative, inquisitive, entertaining and downright funny. It is an exhausting but rewarding beat and I'm glad to cover it with them.

I will forever be grateful to my parents, Mary and Dom, who imparted their own insights into political backrooms and battlegrounds – picked up on the margins of Mum's career working in local authorities – long before they ever thought covering that sort of thing would become my job, let alone something I'd write a book about. Thanks, Mum; thanks, Dad.

Doireann and Bláthnaid Reilly were wonderful writing companions, in that their enthusiasm for snacks often resulted in their daddy taking both a break and a share. Girls, I utterly adore you both.

Finally, my eternal gratitude to my wonderful wife Ciara, without whose patience, kindness, interest, enthusiasm, encouragement and love this book simply would not have happened. Nothing makes me prouder than making you proud.